This
Time

For aaron
best

Jny5

3-00

This Time

New
and
Selected
Poems

Gerald Stern

Gerald Stern

W · W · Norton & Company

New York   London

For information about permission to reproduce selections from this book,
write to Permissions, W. W. Norton & Company, Inc., 500 Fifth Avenue,
New York, NY 10110.

The text of this book is composed in 10.75/13.75 Electra LH Light
with the display set in Candida
Composition by Binghamton Valley Composition.
Manufacturing by The Maple-Vail Book Manufacturing Group.
Book design by Margaret M. Wagner

Library of Congress Cataloging-in-Publication Data
Stern, Gerald, 1925–
This time : new and selected poems / Gerald Stern.
p.   cm.
Includes index.
ISBN 0-393-04640-0
I. Title.
PS3569.T3888T47   1998
811'.54—dc21   97-43670
                                                          CIP

W. W. Norton & Company, Inc., 500 Fifth Avenue, New York, N.Y. 10110
http://www.wwnorton.com

W. W. Norton & Company Ltd., 10 Coptic Street, London WC1A 1PU

 2 3 4 5 6 7 8 9 0

FOR RACHEL AND DAVID

Contents

Acknowledgments

Poems in this volume have appeared in the following books:

Odd Mercy (1995) and *Bread Without Sugar* (1992), W. W. Norton.
Lovesick, Fitzhenry & Whiteside, 1987.
Paradise Poems, Random House, 1982.
The Red Coal, Houghton Mifflin, 1981.
Lucky Life, Houghton Mifflin, 1977.
Rejoicings, Metro Book Co., 1973.

The new poems have appeared or will appear in the following journals:

Poetry: "This Time" and "Both of Them Were Sixty-Five."
Journal of New Jersey Poets: "Self-Portrait in His Sixties."
Iowa Review: "December 1, 1994."
Ohio Review: "Swan Legs."
The American Poetry Review: "Eggshell" and "Lilacs for Ginsberg."
The New Yorker: "Oskar."
The American Poetry Review, Philadelphia Edition: "Something for Me."
The Nation: "Shad."

I

from

Rejoicings

1 9 7 3

The Bite

I didn't start taking myself seriously as a poet
until the white began to appear in my cheek.
All before was amusement and affection—
now, like a hare, like a hare, like a hare,
I watch the turtle lift one horrible leg
over the last remaining stile and head
for home, practically roaring with virtue.
   Everything, suddenly everything is up there in the mind,
   all the beauty of the race gone
   and my life merely an allegory.

This Is Lord Herbert Moaning

This is Lord Herbert moaning and sighing over his lost manuscripts.
This is meek old Blake wandering down the street with his wolf's face on.
Lamb, Lamb is a master—Marvell, Sidney, beautiful, beautiful.
A whole world of lucid and suffering poets talking to themselves.
I dream almost steadily now of interpenetration,
but not with beasts—I have had that for twenty years—
I begin with sanity now, I always begin with sanity.
—After a period of time the old lobster crawls back into his cave;
after a period of time the wise Indian puts on female clothes.
I watch them with love;
my own poor ghost would like to smash everything,
woods and all, cave and all;
I have to smother him with kisses,
I have to carry him from the room,
I have to show him what darkness is, what brightness is.
For twenty years, without knowing the name, I fought against beasts,
but my whole life is centered now in my lips
and their irruptions.
  It is beautiful watching the sun slip through the bent fingers.
  It is beautiful letting the brain move in and out of its own cloudbank.

In Kovalchik's Garden

It is dusk, the drive-ins are opening, the balloon is coming to rest.
Out of the east, so fitting, the cardinal moves into the light.
It is the female, almost too small and shabby for its splendor.
Her crest opens out—I watch it blaze up.
She is exploring the dead pear tree.
She moves quickly in and out of the dry branches.
Her cry is part wistful, part mordant.
She is getting rid of corpses.

The Naming of Beasts

You were wrong about the blood.
It is the meat-eating lamb we are really terrified of,
not the meat-eating lion.
The noisy Soul shrieking and spitting and bleeding set us off—
the smell of nice clean grass confused us.
It is the eyes, it is the old sweet eyes showing just a little fear.
It is the simple mouth full of honest juices.
It is the little legs crossed at the bony joints.
—It is not greed—it can't be greed—it is fasting;
it is not divorce—it is custody;
it is not blood—it is supineness.

The Unity

How strange it is to walk alone,
the one leg never growing tired of the other;

the ears still beautiful but the sound
falling in new places;

all that I formerly believed in
explained and sweetened.

I have to concoct my own past now
out of old inhalations.

I have to live in two lives
with the same blood.

I have to separate the thirsts
without hatred.

It is a good desert—
snakes and horses—

cooks, whores, doctors—
ghosts, vistas,

women and men of all sizes and all ages
living together, without satire.

His Animal Is Finally a Kind of Ape

His animal is finally a kind of ape—after all—and not an elephant,
a release for him, but more than that for the two exhausted beasts.
For years he struggled between them
and it was either the violence of the one or the obscurity of the other,
either way, as it seemed to him then, a concealment,
but now that the choice was made
they could move back into a simple relationship with him, and with each
     other.

What is amazing is the choice itself.
You would expect him to move from elephants into owls
or into the seal-like creatures or into pelicans,
or at least—if he had to go back—back now into hares—
or shrews and weasels, if what he needed was viciousness.
At least you would never expect him to choose the ape again,
not after three hundred years of greed and malice,
but what he was after was not the choosing of new animals
but another collaboration with the old ones,
and for this purpose the ape now more than the elephant
would suit his fever, or what there was left of it.

I remember sitting and talking for hours about the elephant.
I remember the room trembling with belief
and I hesitate, out of loyalty, to do any harm to that beast.
But it is he who will be free at last of *my* compulsion,
and able to graze, and able to panic,
without my interference.
The ape is different—it will be years before he is free:
in the meantime, when we rise we will rise for each other
and when we howl it will be in each other's faces.

There is nothing degrading or cynical in this.
We had to go back again for the sake of all three.

Otherwise we would mix our disgust forever with our dream.
What the ape does is separate once and for all the one from the other.
What he does is illuminate the distance.
What he does is make it bearable.
The leaves sticking out of his mouth, the puffed-out belly, the dirt on his lips,
this I pity;
the muzzled face, the musk-like odor,
this I pity.
I lived and I lived constantly on the verge of a true destruction.
Because of these animals I was able to break away.
I am in their debt.

The Poem of Life

Why should our nation, into whose purses of charity are poured countless dollars, permit the birds of her land, her poets, to suffer scorn and privation? —ROBERT SUMMERS, My Poem of Life

For three days now I have been watching the blue jay take over—
my soul there, shrieking and squalling,
nodding and jerking its head, fluting its tail.
All day Friday it moved nervously between the two maples.
All day Saturday it hopped through the garbage collecting wisdom.
Today it is Sunday, June 4, 1968—I have *marked* it.
My wife and Bob Summers' wife and the little stoned dancer
have driven to New York to look at Martha Graham's old age.
Summers and I are sitting under the honeysuckles
smoking Parodis and discussing the poem of life.
Once he had it down to thirteen words—
the Napoleonics, the logic, the letters of pride,
the six demonstrations, the five assumptions,
all his anger and irony, all his honesty,
his dream of the theater, his terror, his acts of power—
reduced to thirteen words.
—The blue jay is youth, right?—
clawing his chin, stuffing his belly, fighting the dove, fighting the owl,
filling the lawns and woods with his violent sounds.

By eight o'clock everything will be quiet here.
The miserable family upstairs will slam their back door,
the jays will disappear into the maples
and we will have the yard to ourselves.
We will go on for hours,
moving our lips, waving our Parodis,
seizing and judging everything that comes
into the range of our brutal memories,
two delectable Jews,
spending our happy and cunning lives
in the honeysuckles.

When I Have Reached the Point
of Suffocation

When I have reached the point of suffocation,
then I go back to the railroad ties

and the mound of refuse.
Then I can have sorrow and repentance,

I can relax in the broken glass
and the old pile of chair legs;

I am brought back to my senses
and soothed a little.

It is really the only place I can go
for relief.

The streets, the houses, the institutions,
and the voices that occupy them,

are too hard and ugly
for any happiness

and the big woods outside
too full of its own death—

I go to the stone wall,
and the dirty ashes,

and the old shoes,
and the daisies.

It takes years to learn how to look at the destruction
of beautiful things;

to learn how to leave the place
of oppression;

and how to make your own regeneration
out of nothing.

Immanuel Kant and the Hopi

There was a time
when the only friends I had were trees
and the only pleasure I had
was with my crippled soldiers and my glue.
I don't say this aloud
out of any sickening desire to bring back the sensitive years,
like little Lord Christ
over in the Blue House,
but only because I am spending more and more of my time remembering
as my eyes change.
I guess you should weep for me because I am thinking,
like the silk merchants of Easton in their meditation rooms,
and the dead barbers in their chairs,
and the gorillas on their stone seats.
I could spend about ten good years
bringing the things together
that go into my brain,
ten good years on the river
watching the spars and the starved deer and the bathtubs float by.
   Up the street McCormick lies in wait for me,
hoping to help me with my tires and my trees
and down the street Repsher senior burns and burns,
an abused man, living on anger.
I go in and out of this road every day now
as you do on an island.

My house, with its nine white pillars,
sits peacefully on the ground
and I am the strange man
who has moved into the ruin.
From now on I am going to have something to think about
when I drive into the parking lots;

I am going to be refreshed when I walk over the asphalt;
I am going to live on two levels, like a weasel.

It is spring; 1971.
I am looking through my open windows at the Delaware River.
I am looking through the locust trees that grow here like weeds.
This summer I am going to strip some of the delicate leaves from their stems;
I am going to swim over to Carpentersville;
I am going to write twenty poems about my ruined country.
   Please forgive me, my old friends!
I am walking in the direction of the Hopi!
I am walking in the direction of Immanuel Kant!
I am learning to save my thoughts—like
one of the Dravidians—so that nothing will
be lost, nothing I tramp upon, nothing I
chew, nothing I remember.

II

from

Lucky Life

1 9 7 7

Behaving Like a Jew

When I got there the dead opossum looked like
an enormous baby sleeping on the road.
It took me only a few seconds—just
seeing him there—with the hole in his back
and the wind blowing through his hair
to get back again into my animal sorrow.
I am sick of the country, the bloodstained
bumpers, the stiff hairs sticking out of the grilles,
the slimy highways, the heavy birds
refusing to move;
I am sick of the spirit of Lindbergh over everything,
that joy in death, that philosophical
understanding of carnage, that
concentration on the species.
—I am going to be unappeased at the opossum's death.
I am going to behave like a Jew
and touch his face, and stare into his eyes,
and pull him off the road.
I am not going to stand in a wet ditch
with the Toyotas and the Chevies passing over me
at sixty miles an hour
and praise the beauty and the balance
and lose myself in the immortal lifestream
when my hands are still a little shaky
from his stiffness and his bulk
and my eyes are still weak and misty
from his round belly and his curved fingers
and his black whiskers and his little dancing feet.

The Power of Maples

If you want to live in the country you have to understand the power of maples.
You have to see them sink their teeth into the roots of the old locusts.
You have to see them force the sycamores to gasp for air.
You have to see them move their thick hairs into the cellar.
   And when you cut your great green shad pole
you have to be ready for it to start sprouting in your hands;
you have to stick it in the ground like a piece of willow;
you have to plant your table under its leaves and begin eating.

At Bickford's

You should understand that I use my body now for everything
whereas formerly I kept it away from higher regions.
My clothes are in a stack over against the orange pine cupboard
and my hair is lying in little piles on the kitchen floor.
I am finally ready for the happiness I spent my youth arguing and fighting
    against.
  Twenty years ago—walking on Broadway—
I crashed into Shaddai and his eagles.
My great specialty was darkness then
and radiant sexual energy.
Now when light drips on me I walk around without tears.
—Before long I am going to live again on four dollars a day
in the little blocks between 96th and 116th.
I am going to follow the thin line of obedience
between George's Restaurant and Salter's Books.
There is just so much feeling left in me for my old ghost
and I will spend it all in one last outburst of charity.
I will give him money; I will listen to his poems;
I will pity his marriage.
—After that I will drift off again to Bickford's
and spend my life in the cracked cups and the corn muffins.
I will lose half my hatred
at the round tables
and let any beliefs that want to overtake me.
On lucky afternoons the sun will break through the thick glass
and rest like a hand on my forehead.
I will sit and read in my chair;
I will wave from my window.

Straus Park

If you know about the Babylonian Jews
coming back to their stone houses in Jerusalem,
and if you know how Ben Franklin fretted
after the fire on Arch Street,
and if you yourself go crazy when you walk through the old shell
on Stout's Valley Road,
then you must know how I felt when I saw Stanley's Cafeteria
boarded up and the sale sign out;
and if you yourself mourned when you saw the back wall settling
and the first floor gone and the stairway gutted
then you must know how I felt when I saw the iron fence
and the scaffold and the plastic sheets in the windows.
—Don't go to California yet!
Come with me to Stanley's and spend your life
weeping in the small park on 106th Street.
Stay with me all night! I will give you
breast of lamb with the fat dripping over the edges;
I will give you the prophet of Baal
making the blood come.
Don't go to California with its big rotting sun
and its oleanders;
I will give you Sappho
preparing herself for the wind;
I will give you Mussolini
sleeping in his chair;
I will give you Voltaire
walking in the snow.
—This is the dark green bench
where I read Yeats,
and that is the fountain where the Deuteronomist sat
with his eyes on the nymph's stomach.
I want you to come here one more time
before you go to California;

I want you to see the Hotel Regent again
and the Edison Theater
and the Cleopatra Fruit Market.
Take the iron fence with you
when you go into the desert.
Take Voltaire and the Deuteronomist
and the luscious nymph.
Do not burn again for nothing.
Do not cry out again in clumsiness and shame.

On the Island

After cheating each other for eighteen years
this husband and this wife are trying to do something with the three
days they still have left before they go back to the city;
and after cheating the world for fifty years these two old men
touch the rosy skin under their white hair and try to remember
the days of solid brass and real wood
before the Jews came onto the island.
They are worried about the trees in India
and the corruption in the Boy Scouts
and the climbing interest rate,
but most of all they spend their time remembering
the beach the way it was in the early thirties
when all the big hotels here were shaped like Greek churches.

Me, I think about salt
and how my life will one day be clean and simple
if only I can reduce it all to salt,
how I will no longer lie down like a tired dog,
whispering and sighing before I go to sleep,
how I will be able to talk to someone
without going from pure joy to silence
and touch someone
without going from truth to concealment.

Salt is the only thing that lasts on this island.
It gets into the hair, into the eyes, into the clothes,
into the wood, into the metal.
Everything is going to disappear here but the salt.
The flags will go, the piers,
the gift shops, the golf courses, the clam bars,
and the telephone poles and the rows of houses and the string of cars.

I like to think of myself turned to salt
and all that I love turned to salt;
I like to think of coating whatever is left
with my own tongue and fingers.
I like to think of floating again in my first home,
still remembering the warm rock
and its slow destruction,
still remembering the first conversion to blood
and the forcing of the sea into those cramped vessels.

Burying an Animal on the Way to New York

Don't flinch when you come across a dead animal lying on the road;
you are being shown the secret of life.
Drive slowly over the brown flesh;
you are helping to bury it.
If you are the last mourner there will be no caress
at all from the crushed limbs
and you will have to slide over the dark spot imagining
the first suffering all by yourself.
Shreds of spirit and little ghost fragments will be spread out
for two miles above the white highway.
Slow down with your radio off and your window open
to hear the twittering as you go by.

The One Thing in Life

Wherever I go now I lie down on my own bed of straw
and bury my face in my own pillow.
I can stop in any city I want to
and pull the stiff blanket up to my chin.
It's easy now, walking up a flight of carpeted stairs
and down a hall past the painted fire doors.
It's easy bumping my knees on a rickety table
and bending down to a tiny sink.
There is a sweetness buried in my mind;
there is water with a small cave behind it;
there's a mouth speaking Greek.
It is what I keep to myself; what I return to;
the one thing that no one else wanted.

Let Me Please Look into My Window

Let me please look into my window on 103rd Street one more time—
without crying, without tearing the satin, without touching
the white face, without straightening the tie or crumpling the flower.

Let me walk up Broadway past Zak's, past the Melody Fruit Store,
past Stein's Eyes, past the New Moon Inn, past the Olympia.

Let me leave quietly by Gate 29
and fall asleep as we pull away from the ramp
into the tunnel.

Let me wake up happy, let me know where I am, let me lie still,
as we turn left, as we cross the water, as we leave the light.

Blue Skies, White Breasts, Green Trees

What I took to be a man in a white beard
turned out to be a woman in a silk babushka
weeping in the front seat of her car;
and what I took to be a seven-branched candelabrum
with the wax dripping over the edges
turned out to be a horse's skull
with its teeth sticking out of the sockets.
It was my brain fooling me,
sending me false images,
turning crows into leaves
and corpses into bottles,
and it was my brain that betrayed me completely,
sending me entirely uncoded material,
for what I thought was a soggy newspaper
turned out to be the first Book of Concealment, written in English,
and what I thought was a grasshopper on the windshield
turned out to be the Faithful Shepherd chewing blood,
and what I thought was, finally, the real hand of God
turned out to be only a guy wire and a
pair of broken sunglasses.
I used to believe the brain did its work
through faithful charges and I lived in sweet surroundings for the brain.
I thought it needed blue skies, white breasts, green trees,
to excite and absorb it,
and I wandered through the golf courses dreaming of pleasure
and struggled through the pool dreaming of happiness.
Now if I close my eyes I can see the uncontrolled waves
closing and opening of their own accord
and I can see the pins sticking out in unbelievable places,
and I can see the two lobes floating like two old barrels on the Hudson.
I am ready to reverse everything now
for the sake of the brain.
I am ready to take the woman with the white scarf

in my arms and stop her moaning,
and I am ready to light the horse's teeth,
and I am ready to stroke the dry leaves.
For it was kisses, and only kisses,
and not a stone knife in the neck that ruined me,
and it was my right arm, full of power and judgment,
and not my left arm twisted backwards to express vagrancy,
and it was the separation that I made,
and not the rain on the window
or the pubic hairs sticking out of my mouth,
and it was not really New York falling into the sea,
and it was not Nietzsche choking on an ice-cream cone,
and it was not the president lying dead again on the floor,
and it was not the sand covering me up to my chin,
and it was not my thick arms ripping apart an old floor,
and it was not my charm, breaking up an entire room.
It was my delicacy, my stupid delicacy,
and my sorrow.
It was my ghost, my old exhausted ghost,
that I dressed in white, and sent across the river,
weeping and weeping and weeping
inside his torn sheet.

Three Tears

1

If you have seen a single yellow iris
standing watch beside the garden,
then you have seen the Major General weeping
at four in the morning in his mother's Bible;
and if you have seen the rows and rows of onions,
then you have seen the army with its shoes half off
and its rifles half stacked and half scattered in the witch hazel.
But you who have seen the half-eaten leaves of the hackberry
have seen the saddest sight of all,
a nest inside a ruined building,
a father hugging his child,
a Jew in Vilna.

2

You would have to sit at my bedroom window
to see the dog of hay guarding the strawberries.
He is twice the size of an Irish wolfhound
and heavier than a bear.
He belongs to the hairy species with the sheepdog
and the long-nosed collie.
He lies there day after day in the middle of the garden
with his paws crossed under his chin and his eyes watching the road.
He is so clean-smelling and so peaceful
that we forget the strength in his huge body
and the malice in his jaws.

3

I have to lie on my back for two hours
before a certain cloud comes by;
then I only have three or four good seconds
before it disappears again for another day.
What would it have been like

if there had been no maples and no viburnum
to cut off my vision,
if I could have lived all year in the sand
with nothing to stop me but my own thoughts,
if I could have let my eye go freely down the line
choosing its own movement and its own light?

Lucky Life

Lucky life isn't one long string of horrors
and there are moments of peace, and pleasure, as I lie in between the blows.
Lucky I don't have to wake up in Phillipsburg, New Jersey,
on the hill overlooking Union Square or the hill overlooking
Kuebler Brewery or the hill overlooking SS. Philip and James
but have my own hills and my own vistas to come back to.

Each year I go down to the island I add
one more year to the darkness;
and though I sit up with my dear friends
trying to separate the one year from the other,
this one from the last, that one from the former,
another from another,
after a while they all get lumped together,
the year we walked to Holgate,
the year our shoes got washed away,
the year it rained,
the year my tooth brought misery to us all.

This year was a crisis. I knew it when we pulled
the car onto the sand and looked for the key.
I knew it when we walked up the outside steps
and opened the hot icebox and began the struggle
with swollen drawers and I knew it when we laid out
the sheets and separated the clothes into piles
and I knew it when we made our first rush onto
the beach and I knew it when we finally sat
on the porch with coffee cups shaking in our hands.

My dream is I'm walking through Phillipsburg, New Jersey,
and I'm lost on South Main Street. I am trying to tell,
by memory, which statue of Christopher Columbus
I have to look for, the one with him slumped over

and lost in weariness or the one with him
vaguely guiding the way with a cross and globe in
one hand and a compass in the other.
My dream is I'm in the Eagle Hotel on Chamber Street
sitting at the oak bar, listening to two
obese veterans discussing Hawaii in 1942,
and reading the funny signs over the bottles.
My dream is I sleep upstairs over the honey locust
and sit on the side porch overlooking the stone culvert
with a whole new set of friends, mostly old and humorless.

Dear waves, what will you do for me this year?
Will you drown out my scream?
Will you let me rise through the fog?
Will you fill me with that old salt feeling?
Will you let me take my long steps in the cold sand?
Will you let me lie on the white bedspread and study
the black clouds with the blue holes in them?
Will you let me see the rusty trees and the old monoplanes one more year?
Will you still let me draw my sacred figures
and move the kites and the birds around with my dark mind?

Lucky life is like this. Lucky there is an ocean to come to.
Lucky you can judge yourself in this water.
Lucky you can be purified over and over again.
Lucky there is the same cleanliness for everyone.
Lucky life is like that. Lucky life. Oh lucky life.
Oh lucky lucky life. Lucky life.

Malagueña

With a dead turtle floating down my canal
and a stone pillar in my river
and wild jewels growing outside my door,
all I have to do is reach up
and I am back again, living with shadows.

I come from such an odd place
that the slightest wind ignites me
and the smallest tremor makes me weep or lie down.

Tonight, in the dark living room, my daughter is
playing "Malagueña" on her warped piano.
After two weeks of dampness the moist notes
float across the road trying to find brotherhood
with anything that is crooked or twisted or smiling.

I am over here in the garage
letting the mold take over;
I am getting ready for my own
darkness;
I am letting the sound of the islands
go through my veins again, like water.

Pile of Feathers

This time there was no beak,
no little bloody head, no bony
claw, no loose wing—only a small
pile of feathers without substance or center.

Our cats dig through the leaves, they
stare at each other in surprise,
they look carefully over their shoulders,
they touch the same feathers over and over.

They have been totally cheated of the body.
The body with its veins and its fat
and its red bones has escaped them.
Like weak giants
they try to turn elsewhere.
Like Americans on the Ganges,
their long legs twisted in embarrassment,
their knees scraping the stones,
they begin crawling after the spirit.

Gert's Gifts

There were two jokes played on me on my first long walk in Florida this winter,
the English muffin joke and the foam rubber joke.
Nothing else fooled me, none of the grotesqueries and combinations,
not even the driftwood tree growing fresh purple flowers on its green tips.
It's good to be back in Florida where the dead things bloom,
where the sea grapes drop leather leaves in the sand
and the saw grass grows through the cracked cement
and the sweet honeys walk by on silk platforms
promising luxury and renewal in the green darkness.

Stepping Out of Poetry

What would you give for one of the old yellow streetcars
rocking toward you again through the thick snow?

What would you give for the feeling of joy as you climbed
up the three iron steps and took your place by the cold window?

Oh, what would you give to pick up your stack of books
and walk down the icy path in front of the library?

What would you give for your dream
to be as clear and simple as it was then
in the dark afternoons, at the old scarred tables?

Love for the Dog

Before he opened his eyes, as he lay there under the window,
he was convinced he would be able to speak this time and sort things out
clearly as he did when his tongue was still a hammer;
a half hour later he was once again on the chair
with all these keepers staring at him in pity and fear
and giving him milk and cocoa and white napkins.
In the middle of his exhausted brain there rose a metaphor
of an animal, a dog with a broken spine sliding around
helplessly in the center of the slippery floor
with loving owners all around encouraging him
and the dog trying desperately to please them.
He sat there proud of his metaphor, tears of mercy in his eyes,
unable in his dumbness to explain his pleasure,
unable now even to rise because of the spine.
He felt only love for the dog,
all different from the ugly muscular cat
which had leaped the day before on his bony thigh
as if it were a tree limb or an empty chair,
as if he could not run again if he had to,
as if there was not life still pouring out voluptuously
like wild water through all his troubled veins.

This Is It

It is my emotions that carry me through Lambertville, New Jersey,
sheer feeling—and an obscure detour—that brings me to a coffee shop
called "This Is It" and a small New Jersey clapboard
with a charming fake sign announcing it to be
the first condemned building in the United States
and an old obese collie sitting on the cement steps
of the front porch begging forgiveness with his red eyes.
I talk to the coughing lady for five minutes,
admire her sign, her antique flag, her dog,
and share her grief over the loss of the house next door,
boarded up forever, tied up in estates,
surrounded by grass, doomed to an early fire.

Everyone is into my myth! The whole countryside
is studying weeds, collecting sadness, dreaming
of odd connections and no place more than Lambertville
will do for ghosts to go through your body
or people to live out their lives with a blurred vision.
The old woman is still talking. She tells me
about her youth, she tells me about her mother's ganglia
and how the doctor slammed a heavy Bible down
on her watery wrist, scattering spoons and bread crumbs
and turning over little tin containers
of alyssum and snapdragon. She tells me about the
curved green glass that is gone forever. She tells me
about her dog and its monotonous existence.

Ah, but for sadness there are very few towns like Lambertville.
It drips with grief, it almost sags from the weight.
I know Frackville, Pa., and Sandusky, Ohio,
and I know coal chutes, empty stores and rusty rivers
but Lambertville is special, it is a wooden stage set,
a dream-ridden carcass where people live out serious lives

with other people's secrets, trying to touch with their hands
and eat with their cold forks, and open houses with their keys;
and sometimes, on a damp Sunday, they leave the papers on the front porch
to walk down York Street or Buttonwood Street
past abandoned factories and wooden garages,
past the cannon with balls and the new band shell,
past the downtown churches and the antique shops,
and even across the metal plates on the Delaware River
to stinking New Hope, where all their deep longing
is reduced to an hour and a half of greedy buying.

I crawl across the street to have my coffee at the low counter,
to listen to the noise of the saws drifting through the open window
and to study the strange spirit of this tar paper café
stuck on a residential street three or four blocks
from Main and Bridge where except for the sudden windfall
of the looping detour it would be relegated forever
to the quiet company of three or four close friends
and the unexpected attention of a bored crossing guard
or exhausted meter man or truck driver.
I listen to the plans of the three teen-age businessmen
about to make their fortune in this rotting shack
and walk—periodically—past the stainless steel sink
to take my piss in the misplaced men's room.
I watch the bright happy girls organize their futures
over and around the silent muscular boys
and I wait, like a peaceful man, hours on end,
for the truck out back to start, for the collie to die,
for the flies to come, for the summer to bring its reckoning.

The Cemetery of Orange Trees in Crete

In Crete the old orange trees are cut back until they are stumps,
with little leaves coming out again from the butchered arms.
They are painted white and stand there in long straight rows
like the white gravestones at Gettysburg and Manassas.
  I first came across them on the bus ride to Omalos
as we began our climb through the empty mountains,
thinking of the beauty and exhaustion that lay ahead.
They are mementos of my journey south, the renewal
of my youth, green leaves growing out of my neck,
my shoulders flowering again with small blossoms,
my body painted white, my hands joining
the other hands on the hill, my white heart remembering
the violence and sorrow that gave us our life again.

96 Vandam

I am going to carry my bed into New York City tonight
complete with dangling sheets and ripped blankets;
I am going to push it across three dark highways
or coast along under 600,000 faint stars.
I want to have it with me so I don't have to beg
for too much shelter from my weak and exhausted friends.
I want to be as close as possible to my pillow
in case a dream or a fantasy should pass by.
I want to fall asleep on my own fire escape
and wake up dazed and hungry
to the sound of garbage grinding in the street below
and the smell of coffee cooking in the window above.

Bob Summers: The Final Poem

There are two men I know who wander around all winter as I do,
half listening and half falling over rocks and curbs.
One is a bicyclist who pedals all day on
an old balloon-tire bike through Upper Black Eddy;
the other is a bridge-walker who wears a long army
overcoat with "P.O.W." still faintly printed across the back.
There was a third who walked down the streets of Philadelphia,
touching base at the Chess Club and Frank's and the Greek's
like a farmer, or beggar, doing the daily round.
If you saw just the back of his head
and his hands waving you would know he was leading you
through one of his darker arguments;
if you followed him further
you would be dragged to a place where every connection was smashed
and the brain had trouble sorting out its own riches.
I last saw him concentrating with all his power
on the problem of simple existence,
trying to match words with places
and blurred thoughts with things,
reducing everyone who knew him or came near him
to a state of either pity or shame
because of his strangeness and clumsiness.
I remember the rope he carried
and the knot of terror he fingered as he daydreamed,
the knot of release, hanging slack like a crown
over the back of his neck,
always ready to guide him through his weakness,
ready to give him back his health and wisdom.

God of Rain, God of Water

Each spring the long-nosed god of rain,
when it's his turn, rises from the gang of old men
sitting day and night in the dirt in front of the fire
and makes the monotonous noises and does the slow
crawling steps and little bows that are his stock in trade.
Tears pour from his eyes, rheum from his nose,
saliva from his mouth and clean colorless water
in an endless cascade from his swollen tube.

I see him in various conventional shapes in the clouds,
long arms slowly shifting through the light and dark,
or sometimes in the leaves of the two trees,
waving his head and shoulders in the sky
and dropping mist on everything that passes,
or sometimes as an all-night and all-day rain
filling the whole house with dread and sorrow,
or sometimes just as a dirty runnel sweeping
relentlessly through stones and leaves and paper
and down the storm sewers to the river,
singing wildly in the underground passages.

What I do is go around the countryside looking for mosses
or wait for the geese to come back up the river
or stare at the strange red blossoms in my front yard
that are either old seedpods or new leaves on the old maples.
There is a line of sticks I look at on the Jersey side
that I can just see from my bedroom window before my own
trees turn green and blot out the view.
When these sticks grow soft, when there's a slight blur on everything,
then I know the bees are circling the dead logs,
the vines are taking hold in the new dirt
and the first flowers are starting to use the light.

Then I remember other springs
when, in a sudden fit of violence, my own life was changed
in the very middle of its flowering.
I am able to zero in on those years with more clarity now
as each new one passes, so that not one detail is lost;
as if the clarity illuminated the pain;
as if the pain decreased where the clarity took over;
as if the clarity were taking the place of the pain.
—The old man when he goes back into the circle is still weeping
and War and Procreation and Music, three of the oldest and saddest,
slap him on his soaking back, shouting above the roar of the fire
and the constant din of the unorganized gods chattering,
"Nice show, good show, good show," but he, the rain god,
is sobbing uncontrollably, thick drops are coming from his eyes,
and he is gasping and finally his arms alone are moving,
and he is in the center of the huge circle on his hands and knees
pounding the earth, dry gasps are coming from his throat
and a trickle of thin water from his mouth,
while all around him violets are springing up in the dirty cinders,
and giant thistles and strings of chicory and daisies,
to pay him for his tears, to pay the old god for his tears,
apart from everything else, to pay him for his tears.

If You Saw Me Walking

If you saw me walking one more time on the island
you would know how much the end of August meant to me;

and if you saw me singing as I slid over the wet stones
you would know I was carrying the secret of life in my hip pocket.

If my lips moved too much
you would follow one step behind to protect me;

if I fell asleep too soon
you would cover me in light catalpa or dry willow.

Oh if I wore a brace you would help me, if I stuttered
you would hold my arm, if my heart beat with fear

you would throw a board across the channel, you would put
out a hand to catch me, you would carry me on your back.

If you saw me swim back and forth through the algae
you would know how much I love the trees floating under me;

and if you saw me hold my leaf up to the sun
you would know I was still looking for my roots;

and if you saw me burning wood
you would know I was trying to remember the smell of maple.

If I rushed down the road buttoning my blue shirt—
if I left without coffee—if I forgot my chewed-up pen—

you would know there was one more day of happiness
before the water rose again for another year.

Morning Harvest

                Pennsylvania spiders
not only stretch their silk between the limbs
of our great trees but hang between our houses
and pull their sheets across the frantic eyes
of cats and the soft chests of men.
Some are so huge they move around like mammals,
waddling slowly over the rough cement
and into the bushes to nurse their young or feed
on berries and crunch on bones.
But it is the ones that live on the iron bridge
going across to Riegelsville, New Jersey,
that are the most artistic and luxurious.
They make their webs between the iron uprights
and hang them out in the dew above the river
like a series of new designs on display,
waiting for you to choose the one most delicate,
waiting for you just to touch the sticky threads
as you look at their soft silk, as you love them.

If your mind is already on business,
even if your mind is still into your dream,
you will be shocked by their beauty and you will sit there
two minutes, two hours, a half a century you will sit there
until the guards begin to shout, until they rush up in confusion
and bang on your window and look at you in fear.
You will point with your left finger at the sun
and draw a tracery in the cold air,
a dragline from door handle to door handle,
foundation lines inside the windows,
long radials from the panel to the headrest
and gluey spirals turning on the radials;
and you will sit in the center of your web
like a rolled-up leaf or a piece of silent dirt,

pulling gently on your loose trapline.
They will scream in your ear,
they will tear desperately at the sheets,
they will beg for air
before you finally relieve them by starting your engine
and moving reluctantly over the small bridge.

Do not regret your little bout with life in the morning.
If you drive slowly you can have almost one minute
to study the drops of silver hanging in the sun
before you turn the corner past the gatehouse
and down the road beside the railroad cars
and finally over the tracks and up the hill
to the morning that lies in front of you like one more design.
It is the morning I live in and travel through,
the morning of children standing in the driveways,
of mothers wrapping their quilted coats around them
and yellow buses flashing their lights like berserk police cars.
It is lights that save us, lights that light the way,
blue lights rushing in to help the wretched,
red lights carrying twenty pounds of oxygen down the highway,
white lights entering the old Phoenician channels
bringing language and mathematics and religion into the darkness.

Peddler's Village

The small gray bird that fit inside the hand
of a nine-year-old girl is himself a grandfather
with a tear stuck to the side of his round face;

but he hopped on the red bricks and absentmindedly
pecked at her hand as if he were still young and blue,
with oily wings and a stomach full of seeds.

If she could see his heart she would know how terrified he was.
She would take off her colored handkerchief and stop being his grandmother;
she would take away his paper bed and stop being his sister and his bride.

If she knew how old he was she would bow down
and kiss his loose feathers
and listen carefully to his song.

There had to be wisdom with all that age,
something he could give her,
something she could remember him by and love him for;

there had to be some honor, some revelation,
some loveliness before he died;
before the lice robbed him,
before the bitter wire snapped him in two,
before a thousand tragedies took away his warmth and happiness.

The Sweetness of Life

After the heavy rain we were able to tell about the mushrooms,
which ones made us sick, which ones had the dry bitterness,
which ones caused stomach pains and dizziness and hallucinations.

It was the beginning of religion again—on the river—
all the battles and ecstasies and persecutions
taking place beside the hackberries and the fallen locust.

I sat there like a lunatic,
weeping, raving, standing on my head, living
in three and four and five places at once.

I sat there letting the wild and domestic combine,
finally accepting the sweetness of life,
on my own mushy log,
in the white and spotted moonlight.

Underground Dancing

There's a bird pecking at the fat;
there's a dead tree covered with snow;
there's a truck dropping cinders on the slippery highway.

There's life in my backyard—
black wings beating on the branches,
greedy eyes watching,
mouths screaming and fighting over the greasy ball.

There's a mole singing hallelujah.
Close the rotten doors!
Let everyone go blind!
Let everyone be buried in his own litter.

Cow Worship

I love the cows best when they are a few feet away
from my dining-room window and my pine floor,
when they reach in to kiss me with their wet
mouths and their white noses.
I love them when they walk over the garbage cans
and across the cellar doors,
over the sidewalk and through the metal chairs
and the birdseed.
—Let me reach out through the thin curtains
and feel the warm air of May.
It is the temperature of the whole galaxy,
all the bright clouds and clusters,
beasts and heroes,
glittering singers and isolated thinkers
at pasture.

Immensity

Nothing is too small for my sarcasm. I know
a tiny moth that crawls over the rug
like an English spy sneaking through the Blue Forest,
and I know a Frenchman that hangs on the closet door
singing *chanson* after *chanson* with his smashed thighs.
I will examine my life through curled threads
and short straws and little drops of food.
I will crawl around with my tongue out, growing
more and more used to the dirty webs hanging
between the ridges of my radiator and the huge
smudges in that distant sky up there, beginning
more and more to take on the shape of some great design.
   This is the way to achieve immensity, and this is the
only way to get ready for death, no matter what Immanuel Kant
and the English philosophers say about the mind,
no matter what the gnostics say, crawling
through their vile blue, sneezing madly in the midst of that
life of theirs, weighed down by madness and sorrow.

Rotten Angel

My friends, still of this world, follow me to the bottom of the river,
tripping over roots and cutting themselves on the dry grass.
They are all over on the left side, drinking beer and crying,
and I am there by myself waiting for the rotten angel.
For my sake it hasn't rained for twenty days
and all the old jetties are showing up again in the water.
I can reach my arms up into the second row of branches
and pull down clumps of dead leaves and barrel hoops.
I finally find my clearing and fall down in the dirt,
exhausted from thirty minutes of fighting for air.
I put an *x* on the ground and start marking off
a place for the gravel, the rhododendron and the iron bird.
My friends stand above me, a little bored by my death
and a little tired of the flies and the sad ritual.
—How I would love it if I could really be buried here,
a mile away from my house in this soft soil.
I think the state could do this for me—they could give me
a few feet of earth—they could make an exception.
I tell you it really matters and all that talk
about so many cents' worth of fat and so many grams
of water is really just fake humility.
I would hate being dusted on the ocean or put in a drawer
for perpetuity—I want to be connected
with life as long as possible, I want to disappear slowly,
as gruesome as that sounds, so there is time
for those who want to see me in my own light
and get an idea of how I made my connections
and what I looked at and dreamed about
and what the river smelled like from this island
and how the grackles sounded when they landed
in the polished trees and how the trucks sounded
charging up 611 carrying the culture
of Philadelphia into the mountains

and after a day I even understood the English garden
from watching the scattered shutters and old storm windows.
  We here in France salute the English.
We admire them for their tolerance and shyness.
We love them for their geography and their music,
their hatred of theory and their bad food,
their optimism and love of animals.
We in America are more like red squirrels: we live
from roof to roof, our minds are fixed on the great
store of the future, our bodies are worn out from leaping;
we are weary of each other's faces, each other's dreams.
We sigh for some understanding, some surcease,
some permanence, as we move from tree to tree,
from wire to wire, from empty hole to empty hole,
singing, singing, always singing, of that amorous summer.

Modern Love

In a month all these frozen waterfalls
will be replaced by Dutchman's breeches
and I will drive down the road
trying to remember what it was like
in late February and early March.
It will be 72 degrees on March 24th
and I will see my first robin
on the roof of the Indian Rock Inn.
My wife and I will go in to stare at the chandelier
and eat, like starved birds, in front of the fireplace.
I know now that what I'll do
all through supper is plan my walk
from Bristol, Pa., to the canal museum.
I will exhaust her with questions about old hotels
and how much water I should carry
and what shoes I should wear,
and she will meet me with sweetness and logic
before we break up over money and grammar and lost love.
Later the full moon will shine through our windshield
as we zigzag up the river
dragging our tired brains, and our hearts, after us.
I will go to bed thinking of George Meredith
lying beside a red sword
and I will try to remember how his brain smoked
as he talked to his wife in her sleep and twisted her words.
    Where I will go in the six hours before I wake up freezing
I don't know, but I do know
I will finally lie there with my twelve organs in place,
wishing I were in a tea palace, wishing
I were in a museum in France, wishing
I were in a Moorish movie house in Los Angeles.
I will walk downstairs singing because it is March 25th
and I will walk outside to drink my coffee on the stone wall.

Elaine Comparone

I love to sit down
in front of my lilac fence
and watch the wind blow through the pointed leaves.

If I could do exactly what I wanted
I would move a harpsichord into my back yard
and ask Elaine Comparone to play for me all morning.

My friend Barbara Dazzle said she would move
her dining-room furniture out and put the long red box
in the middle of the gardenias and the hanging ivy.

Either way I would listen to the steel bird sing
and watch Elaine shift back and forth on her chair,
torn between my love of Domenico Scarlatti
and my desire to lay my head down on her flowery lap.

My joy begins as I dream of a woman blushing
beside her stone wall, and my pain begins
when she turns into a shadow, with notes falling
around her like blossoms on the wet grass.

I run through the garden shouting kiss me, kiss me!
In one more day the petals will be curled and brown,
they will lie piled up like dead leaves —
smeared on the walk like blood;

oh in one hour the great tree will stand there shaking
and the box will be carried out like a heavy coffin
and Elaine Comparone will sit with her hands in her lap,
in the cold air, rushing back to the city,

remembering the notes falling on the ground
and the red spikes inside the creamy blossoms
and the new leaves making their way like tiny crescendos
in the drawing rooms of Petrograd and Stockholm,
dreaming of sunlight and rain and endless dancing.

When I come home from New York City I stand outside
for twenty minutes and look out at the lights.
Upstairs the shirts are howling and snapping,
marching back and forth in front of the silver radiator.
In a minute I will be up there closing doors
and turning on lamps.
I will take the papers out of my coat pocket
and put them in their slots.
I will think of you with your own papers and your rubber bands.
What is my life if not a substitute for yours,
and my dream a substitute for your dream?
Lord, how it has changed, how we have
made ourselves strange, how embarrassing the words
sound to us, how clumsy and half-hearted we are.

I want to write it down before it's forgotten,
how we lived, what we believed in;
most of all to remember the giants
and how they walked, always with white hair,
always with long white hair hanging down over their collars,
always with red faces, always bowing and listening,
their heads floating as they moved through the small crowd.

Outside the wind is blowing
and the snow is piling up against the pillars.
I could go back in a minute to the synagogue in Beechview
or the Carnegie Library on the North Side.
I could turn and shake hands with the tiny man
sitting beside me and wish him peace.
I could stand in front and watch the stained-glass
window rattle in its frame and the guest speaker
climb into the backseat of his car.

I am writing about the past because there was
still affection left then, and other sorrows;
because I believed my white silk scarf could save me,
and my all-day walks;
because when I opened my window the smell
of snow made me tremble with pleasure;
because I was a head taller than the tiny man sitting next to me;
because I was always the youngest;
because I believed in Shelley;
because I carried my entire memory along with me in the summer;
because I stared at the old men with loving eyes;
because I studied their fallen shoulders and their huge hands;
because I found relief only in my drawings;
because I knew the color and texture of every rug and every chair
and every lampshade in my first house.

Give this to Rabbi Kook who always arrived
with his clothes on fire and stood between the mourners,
singing songs against death in all three languages
at the crowded wall, in the dark sunlight.

And give this to Malatesta who believed in
the perfect world and lived in it as he moved
from country to country, for sixty years, tasting the
bread, tasting the meat, always working,
cursing the Church, cursing the State,
seeing through everything, always seeing the heart
and what it wanted, the beautiful cramped heart.

My shirts are fine. They dance
by themselves along the river
and bleed a little as they fall down on the dirty glass.
If they had knees they would try to

Thinking About Shelley

Arm over arm I swam out into the rain,
across from the cedars and the rickety conveyor.
I had the quarry all to myself again,
even the path down to the muddy bank.
Every poet in the world was dead but me.
Yeats was dead, Victor Hugo was dead,
Cavafy was dead—with every kick I shot
a jet of water into the air—you could see
me coming a mile away, my shoulders rolling
the way my father's did. I started moving
out into the open between the two islands,
thinking about Shelley and his milky body.
No one had been here before—I was the first
poet to swim in this water—I would be the
mystery, I would be the source
for all the others to come. The rivers of China
were full of poets, the lakes of Finland, the ponds
of southern France, but no one in Pennsylvania
had swum like this across an empty quarry.
I remember at the end I turned on my back
to give my neck a rest; I remember floating
into the weeds and letting my shoulders touch
the greasy stones; I remember lying
on the coarse sand reaching up for air.
   This happened in June before the berries were out,
before the loosestrife covered the hills, before
the local sinners took off their clothes and waded
like huge birds in the cold water.
It was the first warm day and I was
laboring in this small sea.
I remember how I hoped my luck would last;
I remember the terror of the middle
and how I suddenly relaxed after passing the islands;

I remember it was because of Shelley
that I changed my innocent swim
into such a struggle,
that it was because of Shelley
I dragged my body up, tired and alive,
to the small landing under the flowering highway,
full of silence now and clarity.

June Fourth

Today as I ride down Twenty-fifth Street I smell honeysuckle
rising from Shell and Victor Balata and K-Diner.
The goddess of sweet memory is there
staggering over fruit and drinking old blossoms.
A man in white socks and a blue T-shirt
is sitting on the grass outside Bethlehem Steel
eating lunch and dreaming.
Before he walks back inside he will be changed.
He will remember when he stands again under the dirty windows
a moment of great misgiving and puzzlement
just before sweetness ruined him and thinking
tore him apart. He will remember lying
on his left elbow studying the sky,
and the loss he felt, and the sudden freedom,
the mixture of pain and pleasure—terror and hope—
what he calls "honeysuckle."

Hanging Scroll

I have come back to Princeton three days in a row
to look at the brown sparrow in the apple branch.
That way I can get back in touch with the Chinese
after thirty years of silence and paranoid reproach.
It was painted seven hundred years ago by a Southerner
who was struggling to combine imitation and expression,
but nowhere is there a sense that calligraphy
has won the day, or anything lifeless or abstract.
I carry it around with me on a postcard,
the bird in the center, the giant green leaves
surrounding the bird, the apples almost invisible,
their color and position chosen for obscurity—
somehow the sizes all out of whack, the leaves
too large, the bird too small, too rigid,
too enshrined for such a natural setting,
although this only comes slowly to mind
after many hours of concentration.

On my tree there are six starlings sitting and watching
with their heads in the air and their short tails under the twigs.
They are just faint shapes against a background of fog,
moving in and out of my small windows
as endless versions of the state of darkness.
The tree they are in is practically dead,
making it difficult for me to make plans
for my own seven hundred years
as far as critical position, or permanence.
—If the hanging scroll signifies a state
of balance, a state almost of tension
between a man and nature or a man and his dream,
then my starlings signify the tremendous
delicacy of life and the tenuousness of attachment.
This may sound too literary—too German—

flat ungoverned tone I have heard in dozens
of museums and restaurants from London to Heraklion.
When she and I talked English her vile husband
frowned and barked at her in his southern French,
and when I shook hands with her to say good-bye
and kissed her on the side of her small mouth
it was like stripping those tiny leaves from their stems
or smelling again the sweetest of all blossoms,
like being again in the Allegheny mountains
where locusts first started, four million years ago.

And that, my love, is a continent and a half away
from Albi, where the northern French descended
on the southern French and in the name of Jesus
destroyed their culture and their strange religion
and made them build a tributary cathedral
where Das Anudas and I walked all morning,
noting every detail of the pink fortress,
fainting from the beauty,
growing hungry from the climb,
changed forever halfway through our lives.

Your Animal

The final end of all but purified souls
is to be swallowed up by Leviathan,
or to be bound with fiery chains and flogged
with 70 stripes of fire.
I walk along the mulepath dreaming of my weaknesses
and praying to the ducks for forgiveness.
Oh there is so much shit in the universe
and my walks, like yours,
are more and more slippery and dangerous.
I love a duck for being almost like a vegetable.
I love him because his whole body can be consumed,
because there is no distance between him and his watery offal.
Your animal is almost human,
distant from his waste,
struggling to overcome the hated matter,
looking up with horrified white eyes,
eternally hunting for space in the little islands of Riverside Drive
and the fenced-in parks of the Village.

I love duck and potatoes, duck and red beets,
duck and orange juice.
I love the head of duck dipped in sugar,
I love chocolate duck with chipolata sausage,
fragrant crisp duck mixed with shrimp and pork.
I love the webs and the heart; I love the eggs
preserved in lime and potash, completely boned duck
filled with ham and chestnuts, fried duck with pineapple
and canned red cherries or sections of tangerine.

This is a poem against gnosticism;
it is a poem against the hatred of the flesh
and all the vicious twists and turns we take
to calm our frightened souls.

The Rose Warehouse

Ah tunnel cows,
watching over my goings out
and my comings in,
you preside, like me, over your own butchery.

I always look for you
when I go back to Pennsylvania,
driving under the rusty piers
and up Fortieth Street.

All of New York must be laid out for you up there,
the slope on Park Avenue,
the moon on the river,
the roof of the Port Authority,

I feel like putting up my own head,
the head of Gerald Stern,
on the side of the Rose Warehouse, his glasses slipping off,
his tears falling one by one on Eleventh Avenue.

I want to see if he will sing
or if he will stare out at the blue sky forever and forever.
I want to see if he's a god
and feels like murmuring a little in the lost tongue

or if he's one of those black humans,
still mourning after thirty years—
some German Jew
talking about Berlin,

the town that had everything;
some man of love
who dug his own grave and entered there;
some sorrowful husband

refusing to wash, refusing to listen to music,
cutting his flesh, rubbing dust in his hair,
throwing in dirt, throwing in flowers,
kissing the shovel good-bye, kissing the small shovel.

The Red Coal

Sometimes I sit in my blue chair trying to remember
what it was like in the spring of 1950
before the burning coal entered my life.

I study my red hand under the faucet, the left one
below the grease line consisting of four feminine angels
and one crooked broken masculine one

and the right one lying on top of the white porcelain
with skin wrinkled up like a chicken's
beside the razor and the silver tap.

I didn't live in Paris for nothing and walk
with Jack Gilbert down the wide sidewalks
thinking of Hart Crane and Apollinaire

and I didn't save the picture of the two of us
moving through a crowd of stiff Frenchmen
and put it beside the one of Pound and Williams

unless I wanted to see what coals had done
to their lives too. I say it with vast affection,
wanting desperately to know what the two of them

talked about when they lived in Pennsylvania
and what they talked about at St. Elizabeth's
fifty years later, looking into the sun,

40,000 wrinkles between them,
the suffering finally taking over their lives.
I think of Gilbert all the time now, what

we said on our long walks in Pittsburgh, how
lucky we were to live in New York, how strange
his great fame was and my obscurity,

how we now carry the future with us, knowing
every small vein and every elaboration.
The coal has taken over, the red coal

is burning between us and we are at its mercy—
as if a power is finally dominating
the two of us; as if we're huddled up

watching the black smoke and the ashes;
as if knowledge is what we needed and now
we have that knowledge. Now we have that knowledge.

The tears are different—though I hate to speak
for him—the tears are what we bring back to the
darkness, what we are left with after our

own escape, what, all along, the red coal had
in store for us as we moved softly,
either whistling or singing, either listening or reasoning,

on the gray sidewalks and the green ocean;
in the cars and the kitchens and the bookstores;
in the crowded restaurants, in the empty woods and libraries.

There Is Wind, There Are Matches

A thousand times I have sat in restaurant windows,
through mopping after mopping, letting the ammonia clear
my brain and the music from the kitchens
ruin my heart. I have sat there hiding
my feelings from my neighbors, blowing smoke
carefully into the ceiling, or after I gave
that up, smiling over my empty plate
like a tired wolf. Today I am sitting again
at the long marble table at Horn and Hardart's,
drinking my coffee and eating my burnt scrapple.
This is the last place left and everyone here
knows it; if the lights were turned down, if the
heat were turned off, if the banging of dishes stopped,
we would all go on, at least for a while, but then
we would drift off one by one toward Locust or Pine.
—I feel this place is like a birch forest
about to go; there is wind, there are matches, there is snow,
and it has been dark and dry for hundreds of years.
I look at the chandelier waving in the glass
and the sticky sugar and the wet spoon.
I take my handkerchief out for the sake of the seven
years we spent in Philadelphia and the
steps we sat on and the tiny patches of lawn.
I believe now more than I ever did before
in my first poems and more and more I feel
that nothing was wasted, that the freezing nights
were not a waste, that the long dull walks and
the boredom, and the secret pity, were
not a waste. I leave the paper sitting,
front page up, beside the cold coffee,
on top of the sugar, on top of the wet spoon,
on top of the grease. I was born for one thing,

and I can leave this place without bitterness
and start my walk down Broad Street past the churches
and the tiny parking lots and the thrift stores.
There was enough justice, and there was enough wisdom,
although it would take the rest of my life—the next
two hundred years—to understand and explain it;
and there was enough time and there was enough affection
even if I did tear my tongue
begging the world for one more empty room
and one more window with clean glass
to let the light in on my last frenzy.
—I do the crow walking clumsily over his meat,
I do the child sitting for his dessert,
I do the poet asleep at his table,
waiting for the sun to light up his forehead.
I suddenly remember every ruined life,
every betrayal, every desolation,
as I walk past Tasker toward the city of Baltimore,
banging my pencil on the iron fences,
whistling Bach and Muczynski through the closed blinds.

Waving Good-Bye

I wanted to know what it was like before we
had voices and before we had bare fingers and before we
had minds to move us through our actions
and tears to help us over our feelings,
so I drove my daughter through the snow to meet her friend
and filled her car with suitcases and hugged her
as an animal would, pressing my forehead against her,
walking in circles, moaning, touching her cheek,
and turned my head after them as an animal would,
watching helplessly as they drove over the ruts,
her smiling face and her small hand just visible
over the giant pillows and coat hangers
as they made their turn into the empty highway.

Dear Mole

Dear mole, I have forgotten you!
Living under the dahlias, making highways
under the pines, coming up to sniff
blindly, like John Ruskin,
at the pink chrysanthemums and the red berries
hanging from the ruined viburnum.

Everything depends on your sponginess,
the world you created with your
shoulders and claws,
the long tunnels and the quiet rooms
where you can wander—like Ruskin—
dreaming of smooth floors and vaulted ceilings.

He was like you,
always cramming and ramming, spluttering in disgust,
hating repression, living apart from others,
adoring mountains, drifting with the vortices,
hemorrhaging a little,
loving high sounds, loving the crystal orders.

He was like you,
following the laws of the fourteenth century,
envious of the fish,
curiously breathless and obsessed with shadows,
loving small girls, living deep in Hell,
always beginning, always starting over,
his head down, his poor soul warbling and wailing.

The Roar

That was the last time I would walk up those five
flights with a woman in tow, standing
in the hall patiently trying my keys,
listening to my heart pounding from the climb.

And the last time I would sit in front of the
refrigerator, drinking white wine and asking
questions, and lecturing—like a spider—
and rubbing my hand through my hair—like a priest.

Look at me touch the burning candle
with my bare palm and press a rusty knife
against my left eyelid while she undresses.

Look at me rise through the cool airshaft
and snore at the foot of the bed with one hand
on her knee and one hand touching the white floor,

the red and blue beacon of Empire
just beyond those little houses
as familiar now as my crippled birch

and the endless roar out there
as sweet as my own roar
in my other dream, on the cold and empty river.

For Night to Come

I am giving instructions to my monkey
on how to plant a pine tree. I am telling
him to water the ground for hours before
he starts to dig and I am showing him
how to twist the roots so the limbs will bend
in the right direction.
                           He is weeping
because of the sweet air, and remembering
our canoe trip, and how we went swimming
on Mother's Day. And I am remembering
the holiness and how we stopped talking
after we left Route 30. I show him the tree
with the two forks and the one with the
stubs and the one with the orange moss
underneath, and we make our nest in a clearing
where the wind makes hissing noises and the sun
goes through our heavy clothes.
                                 All morning we lie
on our backs, holding hands, listening to birds,
and making little ant hills in the sand.
He shakes a little, maybe from the cold,
maybe a little from memory,
maybe from dread. I think we are lost,
only a hundred yards from the highway,
and we will have to walk around in fear,
or separate and look for signs before
we find it again.
                    We pick a small green tree,
thick with needles and cones and dangling roots,
and put it in the trunk on top of the blanket,
and straighten the branches out, and smooth the hairs.
All the way back we will be teary and helpless,
loving each other in the late afternoon,

and only when we have made the first cut
and done the dance
and poured in the two bushels of humus
and the four buckets of water
and mixed it in with dirt and tramped it all down
and arranged and rearranged the branches
will we lie back and listen to the chimes
and stop our shaking
and close our eyes a little
and wait for night to come
so we can watch the stars together,
like the good souls we are,
a hairy man and a beast
hugging each other in the white grass.

Here I Am Walking

Here I am walking between Ocean and Neptune,
sinking my feet in mile after mile of wet life.
I am practically invisible
in the face of all this clutter,
either straying near the benches over the buried T-shirts
or downhill in the graveyard
where the burned families are sleeping in the sun
or eating dry lunch among the corpses.
I will finish walking in two hours
and eat my sandwich in the little park
beside the iron Methodist.
This is the first step.
Tomorrow I will start again in Barnegat
and make my way toward Holgate or Ventnor.
This is something different
than it was even five years ago.
I have a second past to rake over
and search through—another 2,000 miles of seashore
to account for.
—I am still making my mind up
between one of those art deco hotels
in Miami Beach, a little back room on a court
where you could almost be in Cuba or
Costa Rica of the sweet flesh, and
a wooden shack in one of the mosquito marshes
in Manahawkin or the Outer Banks.
I am planning my cup of tea
and my sweet biscuit,
or my macaroni soup
and my can of sardines.
If I spent the morning washing shirts
I would read for two hours
before I slept through the afternoon.

If I walked first, or swam,
I might feel like writing down words
before I went in for coffee, or more hot water.
I will sit on the black rocks
to make my connections,
near the small basin of foam.
I will look at the footprints
going in and out of the water
and dream up a small blue god to talk to.
I will be just where I was
twenty-five years ago,
breathing in salt,
snorting like a prophet,
turning over the charred wood;
just where I was then,
getting rid of baggage,
living in dreams,
finding a way to change, or sweeten, my clumsy life.

I V

from

Paradise Poems

1 9 8 4

The Dancing

In all these rotten shops, in all this broken furniture
and wrinkled ties and baseball trophies and coffee pots
I have never seen a postwar Philco
with the automatic eye
nor heard Ravel's "Bolero" the way I did
in 1945 in that tiny living room
on Beechwood Boulevard, nor danced as I did
then, my knives all flashing, my hair all streaming,
my mother red with laughter, my father cupping
his left hand under his armpit, doing the dance
of old Ukraine, the sound of his skin half drum,
half fart, the world at last a meadow,
the three of us whirling and singing, the three of us
screaming and falling, as if we were dying,
as if we could never stop—in 1945—
in Pittsburgh, beautiful filthy Pittsburgh, home
of the evil Mellons, 5,000 miles away
from the other dancing—in Poland and Germany—
oh God of mercy, oh wild God.

Orange Roses

I am letting two old roses stand for everything I believe in.
I am restricting the size of the world, keeping it inside that plastic pot.
This is like Greece, the roses sitting in the hot sun,
the leaves exhausted,
the blue sky surrounding them.

I reach my fingers inside the dirt
and slowly scrape the sides.
One more flower will bloom the rest of this month,
probably symbolizing the last breath left
after a lifetime of tearful singing.

The wall in back of me is no part of this.
It shows only a large shadow overcome with thought.
It shows him in ruins,
his body spread out in all directions,
his pencil uprooted, his own orange roses dark and hidden.

Picking the Roses

I am picking the roses for next time,
Little Darlings for the side of the house,
Tiffany and Lilli Marlene for the hot slope
where the strawberries used to be.
I am doing this in early February
before the ice cracks and the island gets back its dignity.
There is a towel against the front door
to keep the wind out
and newspapers squeezed into the holes
so we can have good reading for the bright wasps.
If there is a boar, he is outside snorting.
We will need him for the bleeding and regeneration to come.

Soon the dead plants will arrive by mail,
the roses in corrugated paper, their roots packed
in excelsior and moss,
the lilies in plastic bags, *their* roots like radishes,
a leaf or two to signify the good life of the future.
When the time comes I will walk outside to hear my name
ring through the trees, or stop for a minute to hear the words skip
on the water or collect like mice behind the garbage cans.
I will tear the ground with my shovel
and bark with pain as I bend down over the roots
and get ready for the dirty water and the dust.

Then for two blocks up and two blocks down
my screams, and the screams of the boar,
will mix together.
There will be talking afterwards and sobbing
and touches of cynicism and histrionics
in the living rooms by the river,
and single voices wailing in the tradition
of the old Orient, and choruses of flies
boring everybody with their small details,

crash of bone against bone,
mixture of broken weapons and falling shadows.

I will clean up
like a ghost at my own funeral.
My poor left eye will be closed shut
behind its puffy hill
and my right thigh will be permanently twisted.
I will sleep my sleep
on top of the mohair sofa,
over the *Inquirer* and the white espresso.
In one month
the twigs will be shining
and I will be rocking in my metal chair
or sitting on my swing
in the little room on the side porch.
One arm I'll hold up in the snake position
above my head
and one arm I'll hold out like a hairy fox
waiting to spring.
I will collect all the stupidity and sorrow
of the universe in one place
and wait—like everyone else—
for the first good signs,
the stems to turn green,
the buds to swell and redden,
the clouds to fall, the trees to bend,
the tenors of all 3,000 counties
to tremble in the grass,
to beat their chests, to tear their shirts,
to stumble against the sopranos, to rise and fall
like birds in the muddy grass,
like heavy birds in last year's muddy grass.

In Memory of W. H. Auden

I am going over my early rages again,
my first laments and ecstasies,
my old indictments and spiritualities.
I am standing, like Schiller, in front of Auden's door
waiting for his carved face to let me in.
In my hand is *The Poem of My Heart* I dragged
from one ruined continent to the other,
all my feelings slipping out on the sidewalk.
It was warm and hopeful in his small cave
waiting for the right word to descend
but it was cold and brutal outside on Fourth Street
as I walked back to the Seventh Avenue subway,
knowing, as I reached the crowded stairway,
that I would have to wait for ten more years
or maybe twenty more years for the first riches
to come my way, and knowing that the stick
of that old Prospero would never rest
on my poor head, dear as he was with his robes
and his books of magic, good and wise as he was
in his wrinkled suit and his battered slippers.
—Oh good and wise, but not enough to comfort me,
so loving was he with his other souls.
I had to wait like clumsy Caliban,
a sucker for every vagueness and degeneration.
I had to find my own way back, I had to
free myself, I had to find my own pleasure
in my own sweet cave, with my own sweet music.
    Once a year, later even once a month,
I stood on the shores of Bleecker and Horatio
waving good-bye to that ship all tight and yare
and that great wizard, bobbing up and down
like a dreaming sailor out there, disappearing
just as he came, only this time his face more weary

and his spirit more grave than when he first arrived
to take us prisoner on our own small island,
that poet I now could talk to, that wrinkled priest
whose neck I'd hang on, that magician
who could release me now, whom I release and remember.

Romania, Romania

I stand like some country crow across the street
from the Romanian Synagogue on Rivington Street
singing songs about Moldavia and Bukovina.
I am a walking violin, screeching
a little at the heights, vibrating a little
at the depths, plucking sadly on my rubber guts.
It's only music that saves me. Otherwise
I would be keeping the skulls forever, otherwise
I would be pulling red feathers from my bloody neck.
It's only music, otherwise I would be white
with anger or giving in to hatred
or turning back to logic and religion—
the Brahms Concerto, hills and valleys of gold,
the mighty Kreutzer, rubies piled over rubies,
a little Bartók, a little ancient Bach—
but more for the thin white tablecloths under the trees
than for Goga and his Christians,
and more for the red petticoats and the cold wine and the garlic
than the railroad station and the submachine guns,
and more for the little turn on Orchard Street
and the life of sweetness and more for the godly Spanish
and the godly Chinese lined up for morning prayers,
and much much more for the leather jackets on sticks
and the quiet smoke
and the plush fire escapes,
and much much more for the silk scarves in the windows
and the cars in the streets
and the dirty invisible stars—
Yehudi Menuhin
wandering through the hemlocks,
Jascha Heifetz
bending down over the tables,
the great Stern himself
dragging his heart from one ruined soul to another.

It's Nice to Think of Tears

It's nice to think of tears as polliwogs
rolling down your face,
lost on the cheekbones and the distant chin
before they drop on the oilcloth and the pine floor.

It's nice to think of you reaching your hand up
and wiping them away,
all that sadness
welling up, then disappearing.

It's just fantastic to think of sorrow
as water,
to think of it dripping through the leaves
or escaping in the sand,

to see it stretching from one salt island
to another,
or filling the cellar up
and the pools and ditches—

all that grief
where the eyes were,
all that sobbing
where the heart was,

all those rivers flowing
where the swelling had been,
and all those lakes and oceans
where the head was lying,

where the mouth was open,
where the shoulders were bent,
where the hands were hanging down,
where the dark old hands were helpless and hanging down.

Song

There's nothing in this gardenous world more delightful
than blossoms lying where they fall,
soldiers sprawled from one ravine to another,
lovers under a bloody window.

I look up through the branches
dreaming of fate.
My old enemy the blue sky is above me.
My old enemy the hawk
is moving slowly through the string of white clouds.

One day I will wake up at dawn
and philosophize about my state
as I get ready.
I will put on my heavy shirt
and think of the long and bitter day ahead.

It will take hours to know
whether I will live or die,
which car to get ready,
which woods to pass by,
which animal to ride over,
which bridge to cross on the way.

I love the sight of me
rolled over on the ground.
I love being pierced through the heart,
half a man, half a flower,
reaching my hand out, turning my palm away,
one of the many pink and white blossoms,
one of the many on the brutal lawn.

Weeping and Wailing

I like the way my little harp makes trees
leap, how putting the metal between my teeth
makes half the animals in my backyard quiver,
how plucking the sweet tongue makes the stars
live together in love and ecstasy.

I bend my face and cock my head. My eyes
are open wide listening to the sound.
My hand goes up and down like a hummingbird.
My mouth is opening and closing, I am singing
in harmony, I am weeping and wailing.

Christmas Sticks

Before I leave I'll put two sticks on the porch
so they can talk to each other about poor Poland
and wrap themselves around each other the way sticks
do when most of life is gone. They will lie
a little about Walesa, one will dance
and shake his dried-out leaves as if to threaten
the other, one will lean against the wall
as if there were boots to give him courage, as if
there was a moustache somewhere there among the scars
and a thin sword and a thin tear. I'd make them flower
again, I'd make them drive through Warsaw
on the back of trucks, I'd have them reach their wooden
hands through the flimsy slats and take the gifts
and live out the dream of 1830 and the dream
of 1863, the Russians gone,
the Germans gone, the life remade, the flags
flying over the factories, workers dancing
above the trees, a wedding under a walnut,
the food amazing, the last memory the bride's
father in white showing his empty pockets,
his beard a little white to match his suit,
his eyes all wet, his shirt half open—
all that sweetness, all that golden fat—
the fat I love, the sweetness I love—and the two of them
walking home at night after the wedding
talking to each other again about Pulaski
and Casimir the Great and Copernicus
and what it could have been if only sticks
had ruled the vicious world, remembering again
the Jews arriving from Spain, the scholars of Europe
descending on Cracow, half the Italian painters
living in Poland, the gentry reading books,
the women drawing and playing flutes—

forgetting the dream-crushers out there in the swamps,
forgetting the liars, forgetting the murderers —
two sticks in the moonlight carrying on
after the wedding, lifting their empty bottles
for the last time, one of them heaving his over
a sycamore — a buttonwood tree — one of them
heaving his across a frozen river
and listening with his hands on his bent knees
for the old crash, slow in coming, the impact
a half a minute later than he expected,
both of them laughing at the stupidity;
both of them weeping for the huge carp
frozen in mud, and both of them toasting the bride
with broken hands, with nothing this time, with fingers
ruined and shredded, kissing the dear one good-bye
before they go off like wounded soldiers, home
from fighting the Turks at Vienna, home from fighting
the Deutschers a hundred times and the Rooskies two hundred,
home from fighting the Swedes and the Austrians,
two great masters of suffering and sadness
singing songs about love and regeneration.

The Same Moon Above Us

When I see a man sleeping over the grilles
trying to get some heat for his poor stomach
then I think he must be Ovid dreaming
again of Rome, getting ready to write
another letter to Caesar, his third that day,
his tenth or eleventh that week, keeping track
somewhere in those dirty sweaters and coats
of what they owe him now that his labor is over,
now that he's lying there with his hands all grimy
and his face all ruined—

Although I think he is sometimes caught by the horror
as if he had just come to, as if he could finally
let the bitterness take over and just sit there
with his coats wrapped around him, his stinking animal skins
dragging through ice and mud, his mind and body
finally alike, the pedant's dream come true,
the mystic's dream, the lover's dream, his brain
reduced to pulp, his heart surrounded,
his only desire a little warmth, a fire
for his poor fingers, a fire for his poor toes—

I think in his fifties he learned a new language
to go with the freezing rain; he would have done this
anyhow, he would have shouldered his riches
and stripped things down the way men in their fifties
do, only this way he found it easy,
he only had to lift his cold face
from his thin notebook, he only had to look
at the street full of garbage and there he was.
He did have to find another instrument
since flutes wouldn't do and reeds wouldn't do

and the rattle of pencils on the metal grates
wouldn't do—

I see him lying there watching the wind cleaning
the blue sky, pulling a piece of sock
over his raw ankle, asking himself
what he was punished for. Was it because
he sang too much? Was it because
he was too playful, too pathetic? No one could possibly
know him here in New York City outside
the Prince Hotel and the twenty-eight marble steps;
no one could see him with his paper cup
staring up at the dirty ceiling,
trying to remember Love's reception, the white
horses waiting for him, the golden plates
with purple dolphins on them, all that happiness
the one time in his life—

What he thinks he can do sometimes is find
a way to live in this world without rotting
from too much thought, and he thinks he can sometimes walk
past the galvanized soil pipe or the Sid Vicious sign
or even sit all night in his plastic chair
across from the amazing brass ashtray
without half dying; and he thinks he can be an eagle again
and talk to Caesar, and he thinks sometimes, if he's lucky,
he can have his muse back and eat
from her sweet fingers just as he did before
and listen to her song against his lips
as if he were holding the sea in his black hands,
as if, after first giving him all that power,
she now could give him pity and consolation,
now that he's living in horror,

now that his hair is white and his feet are frozen,
she who lives on the side of Helicon,
the muse of luscious sight and lovely sorrow,
he who lives at Third and Houston,
the genius of murdered love—

Although he knows that without this last voyage
he would be only another ruined poet,
and this is his glory—Prince Street is his glory.
The truth is he has become his own sad poem,
he walks and eats and sleeps in total sadness,
sadness is even what he calls his life, he
is the teacher of sadness, there are no limits
to his bitter song, he sits at the long bar
across the street from New York Kitchen
drinking sadness—mixed with wine—
and it is his own regret that moves him to tears
and his own sorrow that saves him—he is saved
by his own sorrow—it is his victory—

And it is his victory that though he lay
bored and oppressed for the last ten years
he sang like no one else before him did
about himself and his own suffering.
He was the first, and since he wrote
in innocence both the remorse and pity
are almost forgivable. It is hard to think
of Coleridge without an Ovid first or Pound
alive in the cage without him. I myself
feel almost happy that he came before me,
that my own wailing
found such a model in his books of sorrow.
In my lighter moments when my cheeks

are dry and my heart is not yet pounding
I like to compare his heaviness to mine —
or mine to his — to see whose chair is older,
whose rug is thinner, whose hands are colder,
although the world I live and wander in
is really not like his, at least not yet —

And when the color south of Cooper Union
settles into mauve or streaky violet
I leave him lecturing his loyal wife
or cursing his rotten enemies
and make my way to the broken-down subway stop
at Spring and Broadway, humming in both languages,
the white moon above me, the dirt somewhere beneath me,
the sidewalks crazy again, the lights in Jersey,
the lights in Manhattan, like the fires in Rome,
burning again without me, I on the edge
of Empire walking west in the snow, my neck
now raw, my feet now raw, my eyes gone blind,
the last one on the streets, the last poet left
who lives like this, the last one who does a dance
because of the dirty ice and the leather boots,
alone in the middle of nowhere, no one to see
his gorgeous retrieval, no one to shake the air
with loud applause and no one to turn and bow to
in the middle of his exile ten cold minutes
before he leaves the street for his soft pillow
and his other exile, far from Rome's domain,
and far from New York's domain, now silent and peaceful.

Leaving Another Kingdom

FOR PHIL LEVINE

I think this year I'll wait for the white lilacs
before I get too sad.
I'll let the daffodils go, flower by flower,
and the blue squill, and the primroses.
Levine will be here by then,
waving fountain pens, carrying rolled-up posters
of Ike Williams and King Levinsky.
He will be reaching into his breast pocket
for maps of grim Toledo
showing the downtown grilles and the bus stations.
He and I together
will get on our hands and knees
on the warm ground
in the muddy roses
under the thorn tree.
We will walk the mile to my graveyard
without one word of regret,
two rich poets
going over the past a little,
changing a thing or two,
making a few connections,
doing it all with balance,
stopping along the way to pet a wolf,
slowing down at the locks,
giving each other lectures on early technology,
mentioning eels and snakes,
touching a little on our two cities,
cursing our Henrys a little,
his Ford, my Frick,
being almost human about it, almost decent,
sliding over the stones to reach the island,
throwing spears on the way,
staring for twenty minutes at two robins
starting a life together in rural Pennsylvania,

kicking a heavy tire, square and monstrous,
huge and soggy, maybe a '49 Hudson,
maybe a '40 Packard, maybe a Buick
with mohair seats and silken cords
and tiny panes of glass—both of us seeing
the same car, each of us driving
our own brick road, both of us whistling
the same idiotic songs, the tops of trees flying,
houses sailing along, the way they did then,
both of us walking down to the end of the island
so we could put our feet in the water, so I could
show him where the current starts, so we could
look for bottles and worn-out rubbers, Trojans
full of holes, the guarantee run out—
love gone slack and love gone flat—
a few feet away from New Jersey near the stones
that look like large white turtles guarding the entrance
to the dangerous channel where those lovers—Tristan
and his Isolt, Troilus and you know who,
came roaring by on inner tubes, their faces
wet with happiness, the shrieks and sighs
left up the river somewhere, now their fingers
trailing through the wake, now their arms out
to keep themselves from falling, now in the slow part
past the turtles and into the bend, we sitting there
putting on our shoes, he with Nikes,
me with Georgia loggers, standing up
and smelling the river, walking single file
until we reach the pebbles, singing in French
all the way back, losing the robins forever,
losing the Buick, walking into the water,
leaving another island, leaving another
retreat, leaving another kingdom.

My Swallows

For hours I sit here facing the white wall
and the dirty swallows. If I move too much,
I will lose everything, if I even breathe,
I'll lose the round chest and the forked tail
and the nest above the window, under the ceiling.

As far as shame, I think I have lived too long
with only the moonlight coming in to worry
too much about what it looks like. I have given
a part of my mind away, for what it's worth
I have traded half of what I have—

I'll call it half—so I can see these smudges
in the right light. I think I live in ruins
like no one else, I see myself as endlessly
staring at what I lost, I see me mourning
for hours, either worn away with grief

or touched with simple regret, but free this time
to give myself up to loss alone. I mourn
for the clumsy nest and I mourn for the two small birds
sitting up there above the curtains watching—
as long as I am there—and I mourn for the sky

that makes it clear and I mourn for my two eyes
that drag me over, that make me sit there singing,
or mumbling or murmuring, at the cost
of almost everything else, my two green eyes,
my brown—my hazel, flecked with green and brown—

and this is what I'll do for twenty more years,
if I am lucky—even if I'm not—I'll live
with the swallows and dip through the white shadows

and rest on the eaves and sail above the window.
This is the way I *have* lived, making a life

for more than twenty years—for more than forty—
out of this darkness; it was almost a joy,
almost a pleasure, not to be foolish or maudlin,
sitting against my wall, closing my eyes,
singing my dirges.

Bee Balm

Today I'm sticking a shovel in the ground
and digging up the little green patch
between the hosta and the fringe bleeding heart.
I am going to plant bee balm there
and a few little pansies till the roots take
and the leaves spread out in both directions.

This is so the hummingbird will rage
outside my fireplace window; this is so
I can watch him standing in the sun
and hold him a little above my straining back,
so I can reach my own face up to his
and let him drink the sugar from my lips.

This is so I can lie down on the couch
beside the sea horse and the glass elephant,
so I can touch the cold wall above me
and let the yellow light go through me,
so I can last the rest of the summer on thought,
so I can live by secrecy and sorrow.

Vivaldi Years

I lay forever, didn't I, behind those old windows,
listening to Bach and resurrecting my life.
I slept sometimes for thirty or forty minutes
while the violins shrieked and the cellos trembled.
It was a crazy youth, wasn't it, letting
my mind soar like that, giving myself
up to poetry the way I did.
It was a little like Goethe's, wasn't it,
a little like Eugene O'Neill's, one joyous
sadness after another. That was the everlasting
life, wasn't it. The true world without end.

Moscow

FOR DIANE FREUND

I love to bend down over my love,
my crayon at her breast, my lips just over her neck.
I love her eyes following my left hand,
her fingers rubbing the Greek blanket.
I love the sunlight on the cold windows,
the horns of Scriabin rising through the dreary street,
the carved houses forever on our wild faces.

Today a Leaf

FOR WILLIAM MERWIN

Today it was just a dry leaf that told me
I should live for love.
It wasn't the six birds sitting like little angels
in the white birch tree,
or the knife I use to carve my pear with.
It was a leaf, that had read Tolstoi, and Krishnamurti,
that had loved William James,
and put sweet Jesus under him where he could be safe forever.
"The world is so bright," he said. "You should see the light."
"We are born without defenses, both babies and leaves."
"The branch is necessary, but it is in the way."
"I am not afraid. I am never afraid."
Then he stretched his imaginary body
this way and that.
He weighs a half a gram, is brown and green,
with two large mold spots on one side, and a stem
that curls away, as if with a little pride,
and he could be easily swept up and forgotten,
but oh he taught me love for two good hours,
and helped me with starvation, and dread, and dancing.
As far as I'm concerned his grave is here
beside me,
next to the telephone and the cupful of yellow pencils,
under the window, in the rich and lovely presence
of Franz Joseph Haydn and Domenico Scarlatti and Gustav Mahler
forever.

Singing

I have been waiting for a month
for this squirrel to dissolve in water.
I couldn't afford the disgrace
of dumping it onto the ground
and watching its body lurch and its teeth chatter.

There is such ghoulishness now
that it might drag its back legs after it,
such desperation
that I might rub its shoulders or brush its lips
to bring it back to life.

You who rushed home to masturbate,
you who touched the same red flower every day,
you know how I must skirt this lawn
to avoid the barrel.
You know how I live in silence.

You who knelt on the frozen leaves,
you know how dark it got under the ice;
you know how hard it was to live
with hatred, how long it took to convert
death and sadness into beautiful singing.

John's Mysteries

I've been seeing these tombstone beef sticks
and that umbrella tree in so many cities
that I forget where it is I am,
whether it's Dirty John's I'm standing in line in
with onions and T-bone steaks in my hands,
or Bishop's, I think it was Bishop's, with hard salami,
safflower mayonnaise and two-percent milk.
My own system of perfect retrieval
tells me it's a big-leaved catalpa,
not an umbrella tree, and what it grows
is not cigars, but intricate seed stalks, terrible
to smoke, cancerless, tasteless, drooping and beautiful.
But I believe only in the islands
so I will insist on emptying the parking lot
of the two beer trucks and putting a table there
under the cigar tree, for me and my friends to eat at.
We will take three hours and end by turning
on the lights and leaning back in exhaustion.
We will be so happy about where we are
that we will cry for sadness, cursing everything
and anything from changed emotional conditions
to polluted leaves to emigration laws
that could threaten to end our mysteries and pleasures.
We will keep the napkins as souvenirs
and write, in ink, what it was like to live here
on Gilbert Street and Market, on Sixth and Pine,
in a town in Crete eight miles from Omalos,
a mile or so from the crone and her great-granddaughter
selling warm Coca-Colas on the flat
at the end of the deepest gorge in Europe—
if Crete is in Europe—at a lovely table with lights
hanging from the trees, a German there to remind us
of the Parachute Corps in 1941,

a Turk for horror, a Swede for humor, an Israeli
to lecture us, the rest of us from New Jersey
and California and Michigan and Georgia,
eating the lamb and drinking the wine, adoring it,
as if we were still living on that sea,
as if in Crete there had not been a blossom,
as if it had not fallen in Greece and Italy,
some terrible puzzle in great Knossos
Sir Arthur Evans is still unravelling,
the horrors spread out in little pieces
as if it were a lawn sale or foreclosure.
—I like to think of it that way, him on the grass there
putting together our future, the seven of us,
the eight of us, by the sea—looking at Libya—
this way, looking that way, this way, that way,
watching him with curiosity and terror,
wondering if he'll get it right, wondering how much
it's really in his hands, wanting a little
to tamper with it, getting a little irritated
with so much of it lying on the ground,
wanting it to be as it once was,
wanting the bull to bellow,
wanting him to snort and shake the ground,
wanting it to be luminous again,
Daedalus and Minos, Pasiphaë squealing with love,
the dear Parisian with her breasts exposed,
little courtyards where we could see the light,
little airways and passageways, pretty steps
going up and down, those parapets where friends
could look at the waves and talk about their sorrows,
those giant jars where all our wines and oils
were stored, those paintings that made us remember, those flutes
that made us dance, that put a lilt in our walk—

Our lives are in his hands, he goes through his wallet
to see if he has money to pay the bearers;
he touches his chest to see if he will die
before his work is done, he puts his camera
in front of the sun, he finds another fragment
that tells him something, he is cradling his elbow,
he is touching his chin, to help him think—
Sir Arthur Evans, angel of death—I walk
up Gilbert Street to reach my house. I live
with music now, and dance, I lie alone
waiting for sweetness and light. I'm balanced forever
between two worlds, I love what we had, I love
dreaming like this, I'm finding myself in the charts
between the white goat and the black, between
the trade with Sicily and the second palace, between
the wave of the sea and the wave of the sky, I am
a drop of white paint, I am the prow of a ship,
I am the timbers, I am the earthquake—
in eighty or ninety years
someone will dream of Crete again and see me
sitting under this tree and study me
along with the baskets and the red vases.
I'll walk across here touching one beer truck
with my left hand and one with my other.
I'll put my old stone arms around his neck
and kiss him on the lip and cheek, I'll sing
again and again
until he remembers me, until he remembers
the green catalpa pushing through the cement
and the little sticks of meat inside, his own
wild voyage behind him, his own sad life ahead.

Soap

Here is a green Jew
with thin black lips.
I stole him from the men's room
of the Amelia Earhart and wrapped him in toilet paper.
Up the street in *Parfumes*
are Austrian Jews and Hungarian,
without memories really,
holding their noses in the midst of that
paradise of theirs.
There is a woman outside
who hesitates because it is almost Christmas.
"I think I'll go in and buy a Jew," she says.
"I mean some soap, some nice new lilac or lily
to soothe me over the hard parts,
some Zest, some Fleur de Loo, some Wild Gardenia."

And here is a blue Jew.
It is his color, you know,
and he feels better buried in it, imprisoned
in all that sky, the land of death and plenty.
If he is an old one he dances,
or he sits stiffly,
listening to the meek words and admiring the vile actions
of first the Goths and then the Ostrogoths.
Inside is a lovely young girl,
a Dane, who gave good comfort
and sad support to soap of all kinds and sorts
during the war and during the occupation.
She touches my hand with unguents and salves.
She puts one under my nose all wrapped in tissue,
and squeezes his cheeks.

I buy a black Romanian for my shelf.
I use him for hair and beard,
and even for teeth when things get bitter and sad.
He had one dream, this piece of soap,
if I'm getting it right,
he wanted to live in Wien
and sit behind a hedge on Sunday afternoon
listening to music and eating a tender schnitzel.
That was delirium. Other than that he'd dream
of America sometimes, but he was a kind of cynic,
and kind of lazy—conservative—even in his dream,
and for this he would pay, he paid for his lack of dream.
The Germans killed him because he didn't dream
enough, because he had no vision.

I buy a brush for my back, a simple plastic
handle with gentle bristles. I buy some dust
to sweeten my body. I buy a yellow cream
for my hairy face. From time to time I meet
a piece of soap on Broadway, a sliver really,
without much on him, sometimes I meet two friends
stuck together the way those slivers get
and bow a little, I bow to hide my horror,
my grief, sometimes the soap is so thin
the light goes through it, these are the thin old men
and thin old women the light goes through, these are
the Jews who were born in 1865
or 1870, for them I cringe, for them
I whimper a little, they are the ones who remember
the eighteenth century, they are the ones who listened
to heavenly voices, they were lied to and cheated.

My counterpart was born in 1925
in a city in Poland—I don't like to see him born

in a little village fifty miles from Kiev
and have to fight so wildly just for access
to books, I don't want to see him struggle
half his life to see a painting or just to
sit in one of the plush chairs listening to music.
He was dragged away in 1940
and turned to some use in 1941,
although he may have fought a little, piled
some bricks up or poured some dirty gasoline
over a German truck. His color was rose
and he floated for me for days and days; I love
the way he smelled the air, I love how he looked,
how his eyes lighted up, how his cheeks were almost pink
when he was happy. I love how he dreamed, how he almost
disappeared when he was in thought. For him
I write this poem, for my little brother, if I
should call him that—maybe he is the ghost
that lives in the place I have forgotten, that dear one
that died instead of me—oh ghost, forgive me!—
Maybe he stayed so I could leave, the *older* one
who stayed so I could leave—oh live forever!
forever!—Maybe he is a Being from the other
world, his left arm agate, his left eye crystal,
and he has come back again for the twentieth time,
this time to Poland, to Warsaw or Bialystok,
to see what hell is like. I think it's that,
he has come back to live in our hell, if he could
even prick his agate arm or even weep
with his crystal eye—oh weep with your crystal eye,
dear helpless Being, dear helpless Being. I'm writing this
in Iowa and Pennsylvania and New York City,
in time for Christmas, 1982,
the odor of Irish Spring, the stench of Ivory.

I Pity the Wind

I am taking off my glasses
so I can stare at the little candles
and the glass of water
in pure darkness.

I am letting a broom stand
for my speech on justice
and an old thin handkerchief
for the veil of melodrama I have worn for thirty years.

I am dragging in Euripides
for his strange prayer
and my own true Hosea
for his poem on love and loyalty.

After a minute I fall down dead
from too much thought
and turn to the freezing wall
for an hour of quiet sadness.

I start my practice later,
twenty minutes for breathing,
twenty minutes for song,
twenty minutes for liberation and ritual.

My poem is about the airshaft
and Zoroaster
and the soul caught in its last struggle
with the two-headed cow, father of everything.

My elation has something to do with light,
my misery with darkness,
my secrecy and fear and distance
with neither.

I end up with a pillow
and a painted floor, as I always do,
my head on the flowers, a little pocket for air,
my right arm drifting and dangling.

I end up just humming,
true to myself at last,
preparing myself for the bridge
and the hand that will lead me over, the hand I adore.

I pity this hero,
so in love with fire,
so warlike,
so bent on teaching.

The Nettle Tree

Mine was the nettle tree, the nettle tree.
It grew beside the garage and on the river
and I protected it from all destroyers.

I loved the hanging branches and the trunk
that grew like a pole. I loved the little crown
that waved like a feather. I sat for hours watching

the birds come in to eat the berries. I read
my Homer there—I wanted to stay forever
sleeping and dreaming. I put my head on the trunk

to hear my sounds. It was my connection for years,
half hanging in the wind—half leaning, half standing.
It was my only link. It was my luxury.

Sycamore

It was March third I came outside and saw
for the first time the buttonwood tree with last year's
leaves hanging in the wind like little hearts
and one or two crazy birds going mad with choices
in the hideous leftover snow and the slippery mud.
March the third. The branches were more a silver
than either green or tan, there was no fuzz
yet. Spring was still in Arizona, the Sonora
desert somewhere, somewhere in Ensenada,
and we were still gluing our frozen ears
to our crystal sets in Fairchild and Waterloo.
　The lower branches bend as if they were holding
castanets in their hands—this tree is Greek!—
maybe as if they were limp, the left hand is limp,
it is a tree from Greenwich Avenue,
from Fire Island, but the upper arms
reach out to plead for mercy, reach out to bless
us, she is a twenty-arm goddess, leaning
over a little, dancing her dance, making
little obscene gestures to the lord of lords,
a tiny finger here, a whole fist there.
　I open the windows, I pull the wooden strips
away from the sashes, I tear the dirty plastic,
I let the sun in. Soon my ties will be dancing,
soon my poems will be on the floor, I am
old Shivers, I do a turn to the left, to the right.
Where shall I go this year? What door will I open
and put a little primitive iron against?
Where shall I put the bucket? I want to live here
beside my tree and watch it change, the brown
give way to green, the green give way to brown.
I want, for once, to understand what happens
when the skin falls off. This tree is like a snake.

How many years does it live? What does it do
in its sleep? March thirty-first, this year,
is the little passage; we will get on our knees
and howl with freedom, not one of us can bear
to live without howling, we were given voices
so we could scream. I sing a song from Florida
about the life to come, someone is singing—
she is a flute, I am a silver harp—
about the seven openings, the soul
skittering, sacred things. I want her to go
so I can become a tree, so I can bury
myself as Daphne does, she is the one
who understands what it means to be tormented;
she calls the spring Apollo, Apollo tortured her,
he followed her from one bare tree to another.
I call it Apollo too, I take my place
inside the silver wood, at least for a year.
Next March the third I'll struggle out of my skin
like a sleepy girl, my hair will be too dry,
my nails too long, my mouth will start to work,
at first it will be too hoarse, and then too shrill;
I'll see the streets will be empty, there will be peace,
I'll walk to the graveyard and back, I'll walk to the lake,
no one will see me, no one will follow me
with rage in his eyes, with brutal love in his hands.
It is like death, isn't it, living in the tree,
listening to what were noises, feeling those changes
and knowing they weren't for you—I love the bells
when they come, I love standing in a grove
and guessing which one she's in—I'm in—if I were
Apollo I'd turn myself into this sycamore
and reach my arms through hers, I'd do some flashy
two-step that's made for heavy sycamores,

and when we lie it would be like two great animals,
sweat running down our faces, tears down our legs.
   This year when I sit at the table with bitter bread
in my hands I'll stop for one full minute to give
some lonely praise to the sycamore; I'll say,
let's stop a minute and think of the sycamore,
let's think of the lovely white branches, let's think of the bark,
let's think of the leaves, the three great maple lobes.
What does it know of liberation? I'll say.
What does it know of slavery, bending over
the streams of America? How does it serve as a text
for lives that are pinched, or terrified? Were there sycamores
along the banks of the Rhine or Oder? Tell me
about its bells again, those most of all,
the hard gray balls that dangle from the stems,
tell me about the bark, the large thin flakes,
and the colors, dark at the bottom, light at the top.
And I will go on for an hour storming and raving
before I drink my final cup of wine
and shout to the Egyptians—as I do every year—
you are my Apollo, you are my fleshpot, forgive me
for turning into a tree, forgive me, you lovers
of life for leaving you suddenly, how foolish
and cheated you must have felt, how foolish the body
must feel when it's only a carcass, when the breath
has left it forever, as it always does,
in search of something painless; and I'll end
by sprinkling the tree and sprinkling the ground around it
and holding my hand up for a second of silence,
since I am the one who runs the service—I am
the only one in this house, I do my reclining
all alone, I howl when I want, and I am,
should anyone come in, a crooked tree

leaning far out, I am a hundred feet tall,
I am a flowering figure, I am staggering
across the desert, and here I am now in New York
and here I am now in Pittsburgh, the perfect wilderness.

Baja

These tiny Mexican mosquitoes are like lost souls
looking for blood among the white visitors
in their own land. They come to lead us through
some four or five old trees. They stoop to bite
our hands, they make that wailing sound I live
in terror of, they sing in our ears, they walk
between the seams, they reach for the drink they love,
they bend half over drinking,
they walk along the sand and through the flowers,
they look for work, they are looking for work, they pound
on the windows of our casita shouting *trabajo*,
trabajo, casting mournful eyes on the sea wrack,
touching the broken sewer line and pointing
at the broken steps.
                              I catch one in a bottle
of Hellmann's and I let it loose outside
on the little plaza where the Citation is parked.
I tell him, my blood is for you, I tell him, remember
one Pennsylvanian who stopped to talk with the souls
and listened to them even if there was murder
and hatred between us; I ask about my future
as if I were Odysseus in hell
and he were Tiresias, that dear old lady,
or some other dead one, a Hercules or an Ajax.
He tells me, I think, to look out for my own
soul in the years to come, he tells me how long
it will be before I can rest a little, although
what he calls rest it may be some other thing
he talks about. He tells me there is a tree
and a yellow rock and a cloud. I should go left
around the tree, I should walk over the rock,
I should walk under the cloud; it is a Mexican
vision, full of darkness and secrecy.

I thank him for his kindness. Maybe he said
there is a room with terrible noises, tie
yourself to the kitchen table, hold your left hand
over your mouth, concentrate on living
a week at a time, divide your life into threes,
the terror can be digested, take care of yourself
when you are in New York, when you are sleeping,
when you are dying, there is a life to come—
or maybe he said, I love you more than anything,
have pity on me, please help me, take me with you,
I want the chance to live again, I can't
believe how large your limes were, oh I can't
believe how huge and clean your markets were;
take me with you, take me with you, wailing
and howling in front of me, in back of me,
pulling me down, the way they do, a swarm
of spirits, stumbling, pushing; I had to run,
I had to slam the door, I stood there freezing,
blood on the walls where I killed them, blood on my palms,
my forehead foolishly pounding, my two hands shaking,
all alone in the darkness, a man of the heart
making plans to the end, a screen for the terror,
a dish for the blood, a little love for strangers,
a little kindness for insects, a little pity for the dead.

Kissing Stieglitz Good-Bye

Every city in America is approached
through a work of art, usually a bridge
but sometimes a road that curves underneath
or drops down from the sky. Pittsburgh has a tunnel—

you don't know it—that takes you through the rivers
and under the burning hills. I went there to cry
in the woods or carry my heavy bicycle
through fire and flood. Some have little parks—

San Francisco has a park. Albuquerque
is beautiful from a distance; it is purple
at five in the evening. New York is Egyptian,
especially from the little rise on the hill

at 14-C; it has twelve entrances
like the body of Jesus, and Easton, where I lived,
has two small floating bridges in front of it
that brought me in and out. I said good-bye

to them both when I was 57. I'm reading
Joseph Wood Krutch again—the second time.
I love how he lived in the desert. I'm looking at the skull
of Georgia O'Keeffe. I'm kissing Stieglitz good-bye.

He was a city, Stieglitz was truly a city
in every sense of the word; he wore a library
across his chest; he had a church on his knees.
I'm kissing him good-bye; he was, for me,

the last true city; after him there were
only overpasses and shopping centers,
little enclaves here and there, a skyscraper
with nothing near it, maybe a meaningless turf

where whores couldn't even walk, where nobody sits,
where nobody either lies or runs; either that
or some pure desert: a lizard under a boojum,
a flower sucking the water out of a rock.

What is the life of sadness worth, the bookstores
lost, the drugstores buried, a man with a stick
turning the bricks up, numbering the shards,
dream twenty-one, dream twenty-two. I left

with a glass of tears, a little artistic vial.
I put it in my leather pockets next
to my flask of Scotch, my golden knife and my keys,
my joyful poems and my T-shirts. Stieglitz is there

beside his famous number; there is smoke
and fire above his head; some bowlegged painter
is whispering in his ear; some lady-in-waiting
is taking down his words. I'm kissing Stieglitz

good-bye, my arms are wrapped around him, his photos
are making me cry; we're walking down Fifth Avenue;
we're looking for a pencil; there is a girl
standing against the wall—I'm shaking now

when I think of her; there are two buildings, one
is in blackness, there is a dying poplar;
there is a light on the meadow; there is a man
on a sagging porch. I would have believed in everything.

Fritz

This is too good for words. I lie here naked
listening to Kreisler play. It is the touch
I love, that sweetness, that ease. I saw him once
at the end of the 40s, in Pittsburgh, I thought what he did
had something to do with his being old, his moving
to the front of the stage, his talking and smiling. I study
the cracks in the ceiling, the painted floors. I love him
because he strayed from the art, because he finished
his formal training at twelve, because he was whimsical
and full of secret humors. He is another one
I missed—I'm sick about it—there is no table
for us, no chairs to sit on, no words to remember.
He knew both Schoenberg and Brahms, he visited
Dvořák, he studied theory with Bruckner,
he was a friend of Caruso's, he was a friend
of Pablo Casals.
                    Something like terror moves me,
walking on 611. What have we lost?
Does Kreisler belong to the dead? Was that a world
of rapture that he lived in? In what year
did he fix his imagination? Will there be strings
two hundred years from now? Will there be winds?
—There is a bank that leads down from the towpath
and I have walked there a thousand times, each time
half tripping over a certain root—I think
it is the root of a locust, maybe a lilac.
Tonight I am partly moody, partly in dread,
there is some pain in my neck, but I am still
possessed a little. I rush into the living room
to listen to either the Elgar or the Mendelssohn.
Something left us forever in 1912,
or 1914. Now we live off the rot.
I wonder if it's true. Kreisler was fifty

when he came back to Paris, over seventy
when I saw him in 1948. The root
was in the nineteenth century. I'm lost,
I'm lost without that century. There is
one movement left. *Con amore.* I began
my journey in 1947. I wrote
four hours a day, I read five books a week.
I had to read five books. I never knew
the right hand was raised like that. I never knew
how trapped the body was. I didn't believe
you gave yourself to the fire like that, that after
awhile—if the brain was in the fingers—the heart
was all that made the sound, whatever I mean
by "sound," and that we have to start with feeling—
we poor machines—which stood me in good stead
for ten or twenty years, that and Marlowe's
tears, and Coleridge's soft flight, and Dostoevski's
rack—it was the fire that moved me.

Red Bird

FOR GREG PAPE AND MARNIE PRANGE

Now I feel safe,
I've gotten my cardinal back again.
I'm standing in Tuscaloosa,
watching her hop through the puddles.
I'm watching her eat and drink, a brown-chested
queen, living outdoors in sweetness and light
with a loose and rotten sparrow as her playmate,
some common thing not fit to touch her hem,
not fit to live with her in the same puddle.

I have to walk over a sick dog to see them,
and through some bicycles and cardboard boxes.
One has a heavy beak and a scarlet headpiece
and one has ruffled feathers and a black throat.
As long as there is a cardinal in my life
I can go anywhere; she was the bird
that, as it turned out, freed me fifteen years
ago in a town in western Pennsylvania
in some unbearable secret rite involving
a withered pear tree and a patented furnace.
There is a pear tree here too, just to add
a little mistiness, and a truck, and a car,
waiting beside the puddle like two kind horses.
But the cardinal now is sweeter and more whimsical
than the last time, maybe a little smaller, and gentler.
I talk and the sparrow flies away, for God knows
what kind of seed or God knows from what kind of shadow.
Someone will say, as he always does, this sparrow
is English, you know, you have to make a distinction
between him and our own, he is the sloppiest
sparrow of all, he is aggressive and promiscuous,
just as he lands on the pear tree, just as he lands
on the roof of the truck, and someone will say, it is

a female cardinal, the male is redder, his chest
is bigger and brighter, just as she lands on the car
and just as she disappears, a little speck
somewhere, a kind of messenger, her throat
abounding with information, little farewells
to the English sparrow, little bows to the scholars
with bird-stuff on their brains and beautiful cries—
something between a metallic chirp and a whistle—
to the one from Pennsylvania, the one who loves her.

Adler

'The Jewish King Lear is getting ready
for some kind of horror—he is whispering
in the ears of Regan and Goneril: I know
the past, I know the future, my little hovel

will be in Pennsylvania, I will be
an old man eating from a newspaper,
I will stop to read the news, my fish
will soak the petty world up, it will stretch

from Sears on the left to Gimbels on the right,
my table will be a crate and I will cover
the little spaces with tape, it is enough
for my thin elbows. They will look at him

with hatred reminiscent of the Plains
of Auschwitz—Buchenwald—and drive him mad
an inch at a time. Nothing either in England
or Germany could equal his ferocity,

could equal his rage, even if the Yiddish
could make you laugh. There is a famous picture
of a German soldier plucking a beard; I think
of gentle Gloucester every time I see

that picture. There is a point where even Yiddish
becomes a tragic tongue and even Adler
can make you weep. They sit in their chairs for hours
to hear him curse his God; he looks at the dust

and asks, What have I done, what have I done,
for Him to turn on me; that audience murmurs,

Daughters, Daughters, it cries for the sadness that came
to all of them in America. King Lear,

may the Lord keep him, hums in agony,
he is a monster of suffering, so many holes
that he is more like a whistle than like a king,
and yet when sometimes he comes across the stage

crowned with burdocks and nettles and cuckoo flowers
we forget it is Adler, we are so terrified,
we are so touched by pity. It is said
that Isadora Duncan came to worship him,

that John Barrymore came to study his acting,
that when he died they carried his coffin around
from theater to theater, that people mourned in the streets,
that he lay in a Windsor tie and a black silk coat.

One time he carried Cordelia around in his arms
he almost forgot his words, he was so moved
by his own grief, there were tears and groans
for him when they remembered his misfortune.

I thank God they were able to weep
and wring their hands for Lear, and sweet Cordelia,
that it happened almost forty years
before our hell, that there was still time then

to walk out of the theater in the sunlight
and discuss tragedy on the bright sidewalk
and live a while by mercy and innocence
with a king like Adler keeping the tremors alive

in their voices and the tears brimming in their eyes.
Thank God they died so early, that they were buried
one at a time, each with his own service,
that they were not lined up beside the trucks

or the cattle cars. I think when they saw him put
a feather over her lips they were relieved
to see her dead. I think they knew her life
was the last claim against him — the last delusion,

one or two would say. Now he was free,
now he was fully changed, he was *created*,
which is something they could have to talk about
going back to their stairways and their crowded tables

with real streaks of remorse on their faces —
more than forty years, almost fifty,
before the dead were dragged from their places
and dumped on the ground or put in orderly piles —

I think they used a broom on the charred faces
to see if there was breath — and a match or two
was dropped on the naked bodies. For the sake of art
there always was a German or Ukrainian

walking around like a dignified Albany,
or one made sad repentant noises like Kent
and one was philosophical like Edgar,
giving lectures to the burning corpses,

those with gold in their mouths, and those with skin
the color of yellow roses, and those with an arm

or a hand that dropped affectionately on another,
and those whose heads were buried, and those whose black tongues—

as if there were mountains, as if there were cold water
flowing through the ravines, as if there were wine cups
sitting on top of the barrels, as if there were flowers—
still sang in bitterness, still wept and warbled in sorrow.

The Expulsion

I'm working like a dog here, testing my memory,
my mouth is slightly open, my eyes are closed,
my hand is lying under the satin pillow.
My subject is loss, the painter is Masaccio,
the church is the Church of the Carmine, the narrow panel
is on the southwest wall, I make a mouth
like Adam, I make a mouth like Eve, I make
a sword like the angel's. Or Schubert; I hear him howling
too, there is a touch of the Orient
throughout the great C Major. I'm thinking again
of poor Jim Wright and the sheet of tissue paper
he sent me. Lament, lament, for the underlayer
of wallpaper, circa 1935.
Lament for the Cretans, how did they disappear?
Lament for Hannibal. I'm standing again
behind some wires, there are some guns, my hand
is drawing in the eyes, I'm making the stripes,
I'm lying alone with water falling down
the left side of my face. That was our painting.
We stood in line to see it, we loved the cry
that came from Eve's black mouth, we loved the grief
of her slanted eyes, we loved poor Adam's face
half buried in his hands, we loved the light
on the shoulder and thighs, we loved the shadows, we loved
the perfect sense of distance. Lament, lament,
for my sister. It took ten years for the flesh to go,
she would be twenty then, she would be sixty
in 1984. Lament for my father,
he died in Florida, he died from fear, apologizing
to everyone around him. I walked through three feet
of snow to buy a suit; it took a day
to get to the airport. Lament, lament. He had
thirty-eight suits, and a bronze coffin; he lay

with his upper body showing, a foot of carpet.
He came to America in 1905, huge wolves
snapped at the horse's legs, the snow was on the ground
until the end of April. The angel is red,
her finger is pointing, she floats above the gate,
her face is cruel, she isn't like the angels
of Blake, or Plato, she is an angry mother,
her wings are firm. Lament, lament, my father
and I are leaving Paradise, an angel
is shouting, my hand is on my mouth, my father
is on the edge of his bed, he uses a knife
for a shoe horn, he is in Pittsburgh, the sky is black,
the air is filthy, he bends half over to squeeze
his foot into his shoe, his eyes are closed,
he's moaning. I miss our paradise, the pool
of water, the flowers. Our lives are merging, our shoes
are not that different. The angel is rushing by,
her lips are curled, there is a coldness, even
a madness to her, Adam and Eve are roaring,
the whole thing takes a minute, a few seconds,
and we are left on somebody's doorstep, one of
my favorites, three or four marble steps and a simple
crumbling brick—it could be Baltimore,
it could be Pittsburgh, the North Side or the Hill.
Inside I know there is a hall to the left
and a living room to the right; no one has modernized
it yet, there are two plum trees in the back
and a narrow garden, cucumbers and tomatoes.
We talk about Russia, we talk about the garden,
we talk about Truman, and Reagan. Our hands are rubbing
the dusty marble, we sit for an hour. "It is
a crazy life," I say, "after all the model
homes we looked at, I come back to the old

row house, I do it over and over." "My house" —
he means his father's — "had a giant garden
and we had peppers and radishes; my sister
Jenny made the pickles." We start to drift
at 5 o'clock in the evening, the cars from downtown
are starting to poison us. It is a paradise
of two, maybe, two at the most, the name
on the mailbox I can't remember, the garden
is full of glass, there is a jazzy door
on the next house over, and louvered windows. It is
a paradise, I'm sure of it. I kiss
him good-bye, I hold him, almost like the kiss
in 1969, in Philadelphia,
the last time I saw him, in the Russian manner,
his mouth against my mouth, his arms around me —
we could do that once before he died —
the huge planes barely lifting off the ground,
the families weeping beside us, the way they do,
the children waving good-bye, the lovers smiling,
the way they do, all our loss, everything
we know of loneliness there, their minds already
fixed on the pain, their hands already hanging,
under the shining windows, near the yellow tiles,
the secret rooms, the long and brutal corridor
down which we sometimes shuffle, and sometimes run.

V

from

Lovesick

1 9 8 7

The Dog

What I was doing with my white teeth exposed
like that on the side of the road I don't know,
and I don't know why I lay beside the sewer
so that lover of dead things could come back
with his pencil sharpened and his piece of white paper.
I was there for a good two hours whistling
dirges, shrieking a little, terrifying
hearts with my whimpering cries before I died
by pulling the one leg up and stiffening.
There is a look we have with the hair of the chin
curled in mid-air, there is a look with the belly
stopped in the midst of its greed. The lover of dead things
stoops to feel me, his hand is shaking. I know
his mouth is open and his glasses are slipping.
I think his pencil must be jerking and the terror
of smell—and sight—is overtaking him;
I know he has that terrified faraway look
that death brings—he is contemplating. I want him
to touch my forehead once and rub my muzzle
before he lifts me up and throws me into
that little valley. I hope he doesn't use
his shoe for fear of touching me; I know,
or used to know, the grasses down there; I think
I knew a hundred smells. I hope the dog's way
doesn't overtake him, one quick push,
barely that, and the mind freed, something else,
some other thing, to take its place. Great heart,
great human heart, keep loving me as you lift me,
give me your tears, great loving stranger, remember
the death of dogs, forgive the yapping, forgive
the shitting, let there be pity, give me your pity.
How could there be enough? I have given
my life for this, emotion has ruined me, oh lover,

I have exchanged my wildness—little tricks
with the mouth and feet, with the tail, my tongue is a parrot's,
I am a rampant horse, I am a lion,
I wait for the cookie, I snap my teeth—
as you have taught me, oh distant and brilliant and lonely.

All I Have Are the Tracks

All I have are the tracks. There were a dog's
going down the powdered steps, there was a woman
going one way, a man going the other, a squirrel
on top of the man; sometimes his paws were firm,
the claws were showing—in fear, in caution—sometimes
they sort of scurried, then sort of leaped. The prints
go east and west; there is a boot; there is
a checkerboard style, a hexagram style; my own
I study now, my Georgia Loggers, the heel
a kind of target, the sole a kind of sponge;
the tiny feet are hopping, four little paws,
the distance between them is fifteen inches, they end
in the grass, in the leaves, there are four toes and a palm,
the nose isn't there, the tail isn't there, the teeth
that held the acorn, the eyes that thought; and the hands
that held the books, and the face that froze, and the shoulders
that fought the wind, and the mouth that struggled for air,
and love and hate, and all their shameless rages.

I Do a Piece from Greece

I do a piece from Greece. I haven't done that
for three or four years. I turn the radio up.
I stare at my ties. I pick a California
and wrap it around my robe. There is a shark
on the ceiling above my shoes. Her nose is pointed
toward the door. She is the streamlined body
we dreamed about in the thirties. Her tail is monstrous,
her brain is a pea. I pluck the strings
in a kind of serenade. I raise the bow
above my head and bend a little, my hair
is hanging down. I am at last the musician
my mother wanted. My aunts and uncles are sitting
on wooden boxes, they are sobbing and sighing,
I take my time, I have a Schubert to go.
I have a light beside me. I am lying
under the Sea of Azov, it is a joy
to be here, they are howling. I raise my elbow
to make a sound. I wait for the moon to shine
on the Allegheny. I look at their faces, they turn
the pages, eleven uncles and aunts, a leather
coffin. I start to play, it is the only
way I have of weeping, it is my way
of joining them, my tears were taken away
when I was eight, this way we end up singing
together. I am a note above them, it is
the thirteenth century, singing in fifths, in parts
of the south they sing like that; the violin rises
above the alto, a shrieking sound, we humans
shriek at the end, we want so much to be heard.
My way was with the soaring and the singing.
Once I heard it I could never stop.

This Was a Wonderful Night

This was a wonderful night. I heard the Brahms
piano quintet, I read a poem by Schiller,
I read a story, I listened to *Gloomy Sunday*.
No one called me, I studied the birthday poem
of Alvaro de Campos. I thought, if there was time,
I'd think of my garden—all that lettuce, wasted,
all those huge tomatoes lying on the ground
rotting, and I'd think of the sticks I put there,
waving good-bye, those bearded sticks. De Campos,
he was the one who suffered most, his birthday
was like a knife to him; he sat in a chair
remembering his aunts; he thought of the flowers
and cakes, he thought of the sideboard crowded with gifts.
I look at the photo of Billie Holiday;
I turn the lightbulb on and off. I envy
those poets who loved their childhood, those who remember
the extra places laid out, the china and glasses.
They want to devour the past, they revel in pity,
they live like burnt-out matches, memory ruins them;
again and again they go back to the first place.

De Campos and I are sitting on a bench
in some American city. He hardly knows
how much I love his country. I have two things
to tell him about my childhood, one is the ice
on top of the milk, one is the sign in the window—
three things—the smell of coal. There is some snow
left on the street, the wind is blowing. He trembles
and touches the buttons on his vest. His house
is gone, his aunts are dead, the tears run down
our cheeks and chins, we are like babies, crying.
"Leave thinking to the head," he says. I sob,
"I don't have birthdays any more," I say,

"I just go on," although I hardly feel
the sadness, there is such joy in being there
on that small bench, watching the sycamores,
looking for birds in the snow, listening for boots,
staring at the begonias, getting up
and down to rub the leaves and touch the buds—
endless pleasure, talking about New York,
comparing pain, writing the names down
of all the cities south of Lisbon, singing
one or two songs—a hundred years for him,
a little less for me, going east and west
in the new country, my heart forever pounding.

I Sometimes Think of the Lamb

I sometimes think of the lamb when I crawl down
my flight of stairs, my back is twisted sideways
in a great arc of pain from the shoulder down
and the buttocks up. I think of the lamb through my tears
as I go down a step at a time, my left hand
squeezing the rail, my right hand holding my thigh
and lifting it up. As long as there is a lamb
I can get on my hands and knees if I have to
and walk across the floor like a limp wolf,
and I can get my body to the sink
and lift myself up to the white porcelain.
As long as there is a lamb, as long as he lives
in his brown pen or his green meadow,
as long as he kneels on the platform staring at the light,
surrounded by men and women with raised fingers,
as long as he has that little hump on his rear
and that little curve to his tail, as long as his foot
steps over the edge in terror and ignorance,
as long as he holds a cup to his own side,
as long as he is stabbed and venerated,
as long as there are hooves—and clattering—
as long as there is screaming and butchering.

Stopping Schubert

Stopping Schubert, ejecting him, changing the power,
I make it from Newark to the shores of Oberlin
in less than nine hours, Schubert roaring and groaning
halfway there, the violins in the mountains,
the cellos in the old state forests.
When I reach Clarion I know I am near Pittsburgh.
I turn the tape down; I can live off the music
of childhood for a while—I still know the words
in both languages—I am not that different
even today. My mouth makes a humming sound
just as it did back then. I take my comb out
and my piece of paper. I bang the swollen dashboard
thinking of my golden trombone; I ruined
the lives of twenty-four families in those days
sliding from note to note, it was my fate
not to make a sound on the French horn,
to rage on my trombone. I still love Schubert
most of all, *Death and the Maiden, Frozen Tears,*
Der Lindenbaum.
I have kept it a secret for forty years,
the tortured composer from central Pennsylvania,
Franz Schubert.

Béla

This version of the starving artist
has him composing his last concerto
while dying of leukemia. Serge Koussevitsky
visits him in his hospital room
with flowers in his hand, the two of them
talk in tones of reverence, the last
long piece could be the best, the rain somewhere
makes daring noises, somewhere clouds are bursting.
I have the record in front of me. I drop
the needle again on the famous ending, five
long notes, then all is still, I have to imagine
two great seconds of silence and then applause
and shouting, he is in tears, Koussevitsky
leads him onto the stage. Or he is distant,
remembering the mountains, there in Boston
facing the wild Americans, he closes
his eyes so he can hear another note,
something from Turkey, or Romania, his mother
holding his left hand, straightening out the fingers,
he bows from the waist, he holds his right hand up.
I love the picture with Benny Goodman, Szigetti
is on the left, Goodman's cheeks are puffed
and his legs are crossed. Bartók is at the piano.
They are rehearsing Bartók's *Contrasts*. I lift
my own right hand, naturally I do that;
I listen to my blood, I touch my wrist.
If he could have only lived for three more years
he could have heard about our Mussolini
and seen the violent turn to the right and the end
of one America and the beginning of another.
That would have given him time enough to brood
on Hungary; that would have given him time
also to go among the Indians

and learn their music, and listen to their chants,
those tribes from Michigan and Minnesota,
just like the tribes of the Finns and the Urgo-Slavics,
moaning and shuffling in front of their wooden tents.

There is a note at the end of the second movement
I love to think about; it parodies
Shostakovitch; it is a kind of flutter
of the lips. And there is a note—I hear it—
of odd regret for a life not lived enough,
everyone knows that sound, for me it's remorse,
and there is a note of crazy satisfaction,
this I love, of the life he would not change
no matter what—no other animal
could have such pleasure. I think of this as I turn
the music off, and I think of his poor eyes
as they turned to ice—his son was in the room
and saw the change—I call it a change. Bartók
himself lectured his friends on death, it was
his woods and mountain lecture, fresh green shoots
pushing up through the old, the common home
that waits us all, the cycles, the laws of nature,
wonderfully European, all life and death
at war—peacefully—one thing replacing another,
although he grieved over cows and pitied dogs
and listened to pine cones as if they came from the sea
and fretted over the smallest of life.
                                             He died
September 28, 1945,
just a month after the war was over.
It took him sixty days to finish the piece
from the time he lay there talking to Koussevitsky
to the time he put a final dot on the paper,

a little pool of ink to mark the ending.
There are the five loud notes, I walk upstairs
to hear them, I put a silk shawl over my head
and rock on the wooden floor, the shawl is from France
and you can see between the threads; I feel
the darkness, I was born with a veil over
my eyes, it took me forty years to rub
the gum away, it was a blessing, I sit
for twenty minutes in silence, daylight is coming,
the moon is probably near, probably lifting
its satin nightgown, one hand over the knee
to hold the cloth up so the feet can walk
through the wet clouds; I love that bent-over motion,
that grace at the end of a long and furious night.
I go to sleep on the floor, there is a pillow
somewhere for my heavy head, my hand
is resting on the jacket, Maazel is leading
the Munich orchestra, a nurse is pulling
the sheet up, Bartók is dead, his wife is walking
past the sun room, her face is white, her mind
is on the apartment they lost, where she would put
the rugs, how she would carry in his breakfast,
where they would read, her mind is on Budapest,
she plays the piano for him, she is eighteen
and he is thirty-seven, he is gone
to break the news, she waits in agony,
she goes to the telephone; I turn to the window,
I stare at my palm, I draw a heart in the dust,
I put the arrow through it, I place the letters
one inside the other. I sleep, I sleep.

A Song for the Romeos*

FOR MY BROTHERS
JIM WRIGHT AND DICK HUGO

I'm singing a song for the romeos
I wore for ten years on my front stoop in the North Side,
and for the fat belly I carried
and the magic ticket sticking out of my greasy hatband
or my vest pocket,
the green velvet one with the checkered borders
and the great stretched back with the tan ribs
going west and east like fishes of the deep looking for their covers.

I'm wearing my romeos
with the papery thin leather
and the elastic side bands.
They are made for sitting,
or a little walking into the kitchen and out,
a little tea in the hands,
a little Old Forester or a little Schenley in the tea.

I'm singing a song for the corner store
and the empty shelves;
for the two blocks of flattened buildings
and broken glass;
for the streetcar that still rounds the bend
with sparks flying through the air.

And the woman with a shopping bag,
and the girl with a book
walking home one behind the other,
their steps half dragging, half ringing,
the romeos keeping time,
tapping and knocking and clapping on the wooden steps
and the cement sidewalk.

* Romeos were a kind of indoor/outdoor slipper or sandal.

My First Kinglet

I saw my first kinglet in Iowa City
on Sunday, April twenty-second, 1984,
flying from tree to tree, and bush to bush.
She had a small yellow patch on her stomach,
a little white around her eyes. I reached
for a kiss, still dumb and silent as always. I put
a finger out for a branch and opened my hand
for a kind of clearing in the woods, a wrinkled
nest you'd call it, half inviting, half
disgusting maybe, or terrifying, a pink
and living nest. The kinglet stood there singing
"A Mighty Fortress Is Our God." She was
a pure Protestant, warbling in the woods,
confessing everything. I said good-bye,
a friend of all the Anabaptists, a friend
of all the Lutherans. I cleared my throat
and off she went for some other pink finger
and some other wrinkled palm. I started to whistle,
but only to the trees; my kinglet was gone
and her pipe was gone and her yellow crown was gone,
and I was left with only a spiral notebook
and the end of a pencil. I was good and careful,
for all I had left of the soul was in that stub,
a wobbling hunk of lead embedded in wood,
pine probably—pencils are strange—I sang
another Protestant hymn; the lead was loose
and after a minute I knew I'd just be holding
the blunt and slippery end. That was enough
for one Sunday. I thanked the trees, I thanked
the tulips with their six red tongues. I lay
another hour, another hour; I either
slept a little or thought a little. Life—
it could have been a horror, it could have been

gory and full of pain. I ate my sandwich
and waited for a signal, then I began
my own confession; I walked on the stones, I sighed
under a hemlock, I whistled under a pine,
and reached my own house almost out of breath
from walking too fast—from talking too loud—
from waving my arms and beating my palms; I was,
for five or ten minutes, one of those madmen you see
forcing their way down Broadway, reasoning with themselves
the way a squirrel does, the way a woodpecker does,
half dressed in leaf, half dressed in light, my dear face
appearing and disappearing, my heavy legs
with their shortened hamstrings tripping a little, a yard
away from my wooden steps and my rusty rail,
the thicket I lived in for two years, more or less,
Dutch on one side, American Sioux on the other,
Puerto Rican and Bronx Hasidic inside,
a thicket fit for a king or a wandering kinglet.

There I Was One Day

There I was one day
in the parking lot of the First Brothers' Church
on one foot, a giant whooping crane
with my left ibex finger against my temple
trying to remember what my theory of corruption was
and why I got so angry years ago
at my poor mother and father, immigrant cranes
from Polish Russia and German and Jewish Ukraine—
the good days then, hopping both ways like a frog,
and croaking, and trying to remember why it was
I soothed myself with words
at that flimsy secretary, not meant for knees,
not meant for a soul, not least a human one,
and trying to remember how I pieced together
the great puzzle, and how delighted I was
I would never again be bitten twice,
on either hand, the left one or the other.
I stopped between the telephone pole and the ivy
and sang to myself. I do it now for pleasure.
I thought I'd trace the line of pure decadence
to either Frank Sinatra or Jackie Gleason,
and thence to either the desert or the swamp,
Greater Nevada or Miami Beach;
or I would smile with Stalin or frown with Frick,
Stalin and Frick, both from Pittsburgh; Mellon,
Ehrlichman, Paul the Fortieth, Paul the Fiftieth.
I learned my bitterness at the dining-room table
and used it everywhere. One time I yanked
the tablecloth off with everything on top of it.
It was the kind of strength that lets you lift
the back end of a car, it was the rush
of anger and righteousness you shake from later.
My Polish mother and my Ukrainian father

sat there white-faced. They had to be under fifty,
maybe closer to forty. I had hit them
between the eyes, I had screamed in their ears
and spit in their faces. Forty years later I stutter
when I think about it; it is the stuttering
of violent justice. I turned left on Third—
it was called Pomfret in 1776—
and made my way to the square—I think I did that—
past the Plaza II and the old Huntington,
and did an Egyptian turn. There were some other birds
sitting there on the benches, eating egg salad
and smoking autumn leaves. They didn't seem to care
or even notice. We sat there for the humming
and later we left, one at a time, and limped
away at different speeds, in different directions.
I ended up doing a circle, east on one street,
north on another, past the round oak table
in the glass window, past the swimming pool
at the YW. Just a walk for me
is full of exhaustion; nobody does it my way,
shaking the left foot, holding the right foot up,
a stork from Broadway, a heron from Mexico,
a pink flamingo from Greece.

One Animal's Life

FOR ROSALIND PACE

This is how I saved one animal's life,
I raised the lid of the stove and lifted the hook
that delicately held the cheese—I think it was bacon—
so there could be goodness and justice under there.
It was a thirty-inch range with the pilot lit
in the center of two small crosses. It was a Wincroft
with a huge oven and two flat splash pans above it.
The four burners were close together, it was
a piece of white joy, from 1940 I'd judge
from the two curved handles, yet not as simple as
my old Slattery, not as sleek. I owe
a lot to the woman who gave me this house, she is
a lover of everything big and small, she moans
for certain flowers and insects, I hear her snuffle
all night sometimes, I hear her groan. She gave me
a bed and a kitchen, she gave me music, I couldn't be
disloyal to her, yet I had to lift
the murderous hook. I'll hear her lectures later
on *my* inconsistencies and hypocrisies;
I'll struggle in the meantime, like everyone else, to make
my way between the stove and refrigerator
without sighing or weeping too much. Mice
are small and ferocious. If I killed one it wouldn't be
with poison or traps. I couldn't just use our weapons
without some compensation. I'd have to be present—
if it was a trap—and hear it crash and lift
the steel myself and look at the small flat nose
or the small crushed head, I'd have to hold the pallet
and drop the body into a bag. I ask
forgiveness of butchers and hunters; I'm starting to talk
to vegetarians now, I'm reading books,
I'm washing my icebox down with soda and lye,
I'm buying chicory, I'm storing beans.

I should have started this thirty years ago,
holding my breath, eating ozone, starving,
sitting there humming, feeling pure and indignant
beside the chewed-up bags and the black droppings.

Silver Hand

There is that little silver hand. I wrap
my fingers around the wrist. I press my thumb
on the shiny knuckles. There is a little slot
in the empty palm—the lines are crude and lifeless,
more like an ape's hand, more like a child's, no hope
for the future of any kind, a life line dragging
its way through civilization, the line of destiny
faint and broken, a small abandoned road,
the heart line short, no sweetness, no ecstasy,
and no dear journeys, and no great windfalls. I shake
the wrist, there are some dimes and nickels inside,
but it is mostly empty, an empty hand
reaching out. It is the hand that acts
for the spirit, there is a connection, the hand has mercy,
the hand is supple and begs, the hand is delicate,
even if it is brutal sometimes, even if it is evil—
and it is penniless and lost, a true
spirit, that sings a little and dances a little,
green or shiny on the outside, black on the inside.
Give to the hand!

Washington Square

Now after all these years I am just that one pigeon
limping over toward that one sycamore tree
with my left leg swollen and my left claw bent and my neck
just pulling me along. It is the annual
day of autumn glory, but I am limping
into the shade of that one sycamore tree.
Forget about Holley crumbling out there in the square,
forget about Garibaldi in his little hollow;
remember one pigeon, white and gray, with a touch
of the old blue, his red leg swollen, his claw
dragging him on and on, the sickness racking
his skinny neck; remember the one pigeon
fighting his way through the filthy marijuana,
sighing.

Bob Summers' Body

I never told this—I saw Bob Summers' body
one last time when they dropped him down the chute
at the crematorium. He turned over twice
and seemed to hang with one hand to the railing
as if he had to sit up once and scream
before he reached the flames. I was half terrified
and half ashamed to see him collapse like that
just two minutes after we had sung for him
and said our pieces. It was impossible
for me to see him starting another destiny
piled up like that, or see him in that furnace
as one who was being consoled or purified.
If only we had wrapped him in his sheet
so he could be prepared; there is such horror
standing before Persephone with a suit on,
the name of the manufacturer in the lining,
the pants too short, or too long. How hard it was
for poor Bob Summers in this life, how he struggled
to be another person. I hope his voice,
which he lost through a stroke in 1971,
was given back to him, wherever he strayed,
the smell of smoke still on him, the fire lighting up
his wonderful eyes again, his hands explaining,
anyone, god or man, moved by his logic,
spirits in particular, saved by the fire and clasping
their hands around their knees, some still worm-bound,
their noses eaten away, their mouths only dust,
nodding and smiling in the plush darkness.

It Was in Houston

It was in Houston I saw this disgusting sideboard
with dogs and foxes and lobsters carved into
the wood, a giant stag was hanging down
from a polished rope, there was an eagle on top
and bowls of fruit and plates of fish—all carved.
I opened the drawer and put my message inside.
The drawer was smooth and faultless, one of the hidden
ones without knobs, curved and rounded, with nice
round insides that soothe the soul. It might
take a year for someone to open the drawer.
It would be either a mother or her son;
the mother would be mad with cleaning, her fingers
would itch to get at the inside of that furniture
and rub some oil into the corners, the son
would long to take the piece apart, to loosen
the stag, to free the eagle, to find a dime
inside the hidden drawer. This would be before
she turned to books and he turned to motorcycles;
or it would be a musician, someone who loves
to touch old wood. It never would be a poet—
they are all blind—who pulls the drawer and finds
my secret words. For any of these three,
here is the white pen I am writing with,
here is my yellow tablet, there are no
magic thumb prints, nothing that is not there,
only the hum, and I have buried that
on the piece of paper. It is a small envelope;
I always have one in my jacket; the words
are simple, half music, half thought, half tongue, half tear,
and made for the pocket book or the hip pocket,
or the inside of a wallet—I like that best—
folded up, and there are broken words,
or torn, hanging onto the threads, the deep ones

underneath the flap, the dark ones forever creased,
the song half hovering in that cloth lining
as if a moth were struggling out of the leather,
half caught between the money and the poetry,
little white one in the ravaged world.

Neither English nor Spanish

FOR HEIDI KALAFSKI

It was when I went out to get an angry soul
a little cool and a little windy. Some bird
was clacking his beak or maybe rubbing his gums
together either for singing or for crushing
a watery insect. I was driving with one sister
to find another and the car we drove in
was huge and fast and dangerous. I thought
the darkness we drove in was something like daylight although
the lights on the body seemed more like lamps, just lighting
the ten or twelve feet in front of us. It is
the madness of northern New Jersey I'm describing,
a sulphur day and night, a cloud of gas
always hanging above us. We drifted down
to Newark, there were clusters of people in front of
every bar and drug store, they were mostly
very young, as if the population over twenty
had disappeared and the care of life and the care of
the culture were in the hands of babies, all our
wisdom, our history, were in their hands. I stopped
over and over to ask directions, the language
they spoke was neither English nor Spanish, they either
pointed in some odd direction or stood there staring.
I bounced up over the curb into a radiant
gasoline island; there was a psychopomp
in a clean white suit who calmed me down and told me
where the phone booth and the park was I wanted.
His English was perfect. I was shocked to see him
in a job like that, reaching over and wiping
the mist away, holding his hand on the pump,
staring at nothing. He should have been a lawyer
or engineer, but he was black, although
he could have been a student. I gave him a tip
and turned around. This time I found the park

in half a minute but there was nothing in sight,
not even a police car with its fat dog yowling
or some stray bleak berserker on the burnt grass.
I locked the car, the other sister sat there
trembling. I tried to smile. I found a dime,
and then a quarter, for my phone call. I stood there
on the sidewalk holding the black receiver
and listening to noisy insects. The sweet life
outside is different from the life of the car.
I suddenly wanted to walk. I wanted to touch
the trees, or sit on the ground. There was a ringing
but no one answered, as I recall. I shouldn't
have made a mystique of that but I was shouting
"bad connection" to myself and "vile connection"
and "fake connection," all that we hold dear
in twentieth-century evil communication.
That was where I could have lifted my fist
and played for the dirty trees, but I was tired
and struggling with the stupid lock, a Ford
Galaxy Superba. Anyhow, I got bored
with the park and its shadows, I did a fainthearted dance,
a mild frenzy on the sidewalk, and sang me
a primitive note, a long moaning note,
as I put my car into "drive," the lever hanging
somewhere in oblivion, the meshes
ruined, no right connection between the orange
letters and the mushy gears.
                                        This was
my futile descent into Newark. We returned
empty-handed, empty-hearted. I smoked
a single cigarette in the blackness and ranted
against New Jersey, as if there was a difference
between one land and another. That dear girl

we looked for would be sitting in the kitchen,
surrounded by her family, thin and exhausted,
full of terror, her mind erasing one horror
after another; and I would hold her and kiss her
along with the others. We would be some tragic
group somewhere, someone would boil water,
and we would talk all night, even end up laughing
a little before the streaks of light and the morning
noises brought us to our senses. I turned
right where I had to turn right and found the buried
driveway as always. I was right, the kitchen
lights were burning and there were cars and trucks
parked wildly in the yard. I looked at the dawn
behind the A&P and the pizzeria—
that takes two seconds in New Jersey—and climbed
over a sled, a tire and an ironing board—
I who saw the dead and knew the music—
and opened the door to that embattled kitchen
and shook hands all around, I and the sister.

Another Insane Devotion

This was gruesome—fighting over a ham sandwich
with one of the tiny cats of Rome, he leaped
on my arm and half hung on to the food and half
hung on to my shirt and coat. I tore it apart
and let him have his portion, I think I lifted him
down, sandwich and all, on the sidewalk and sat
with my own sandwich beside him, maybe I petted
his bony head and felt him shiver. I have
told this story over and over; some things
root in the mind; his boldness, of course, was frightening
and unexpected—his stubbornness—though hunger
drove him mad. It was the breaking of boundaries,
the sudden invasion, but not only that, it was
the sharing of food and the sharing of space; he didn't
run into an alley or into a cellar,
he sat beside me, eating, and I didn't run
into a trattoria, say, shaking,
with food on my lips and blood on my cheek, sobbing;
but not only that, I had gone there to eat
and wait for someone. I had maybe an hour
before she would come and I was full of hope
and excitement. I have resisted for years
interpreting this, but now I think I was given
a clue, or I was giving myself a clue,
across the street from the glass sandwich shop.
That was my last night with her, the next day
I would leave on the train for Paris and she would
meet her husband. Thirty-five years ago
I ate my sandwich and moaned in her arms, we were
dying together; we never met again
although she was pregnant when I left her—I have
a daughter or son somewhere, darling grandchildren
in Norwich, Connecticut, or Canton, Ohio.

Every five years I think about her again
and plan on looking her up. The last time
I was sitting in New Brunswick, New Jersey,
and heard that her husband was teaching at Princeton,
if she was still married, or still alive, and tried
calling. I went that far. We lived
in Florence and Rome. We rowed in the bay of Naples
and floated, naked, on the boards. I started
to think of her again today. I still
am horrified by the cat's hunger. I still
am puzzled by the connection. This is another
insane devotion, there must be hundreds, although
it isn't just that, there is no pain, and the thought
is fleeting and sweet. I think it's my own dumb boyhood,
walking around with Slavic cheeks and burning
stupid eyes. I think I gave the cat
half of my sandwich to buy my life, I think
I broke it in half as a decent sacrifice.
It was this I bought, the red coleus,
the split rocking chair, the silk lampshade.
Happiness. I watched him with pleasure.
I bought memory. I could have lost it.
How crazy it sounds. His face twisted with cunning.
The wind blowing through his hair. His jaws working.

Making the Light Come

My pen was always brown or blue, with stripes
of gold or silver at the shaft for streaks
of thought and feeling. I always wore the nib
on the left side. I was a mirror right-hander,
not a crazy twisted left-handed cripple,
trying to live in this world, his wrist half broken,
his shoulder shot through with pain. I lived by smiling,
I turned my face to the light—a frog does that,
not only a bird—and changed my metal table
three or four times. I struggled for rights to the sun
not only because of the heat. I wanted to see
the shadows on the wall, the trees and vines,
and I wanted to see the white wisteria
hanging from the roof. To sit half under it.
Light was my information. I was an immigrant
Jew in Boston, I was a Vietnamese
in San Jose, taking a quick lunch hour,
reading Browning—how joyous—I was worshiping
light three dozen years ago, it led me
astray, I never saw it was a flower
and darkness was the seed; I never potted
the dirt and poured the nutriments, I never
waited week after week for the smallest gleam.
I sit in the sun forgiving myself; I know
exactly when to dig. What other poet
is on his knees in the frozen clay with a spade
and a silver fork, fighting the old maples,
scattering handfuls of gypsum and moss, still worshiping?

It Was a Rising

It was a rising that brought the worms. They came
when the bodies came, the air was muddy, it was
a small mistake, the fingers were gone, the lips
were eaten away—though I love worms, they have
bags on their backs and pointed sticks, they come
by the thousands, they can clean a beach in an hour,
they can clean the ground of fruit and bottles,
paper and plastic. I was a worm once, I wore
an olive uniform, my specialty was Luckies,
I speared them by threes, I hooked a bone to a cup,
I caught the silver foil. The rain when it comes
forces the worms to the surface; that is another
rising but not as cataclysmic. Love
of one thing for another brought them up,
and love will bring them back. This is the flesh
that dies and this is the flesh that lives. The bone
at the base of the spine is called the almond, it is
the nucleus of our birth. I had my chance
when the worms were in the air. I went out swimming,
I started to float, I held my arms up sideways
and let myself be eaten. I lie on the beach
planning my future. I am a mile away
from the motors out there and I am a yard away
from the wet footprints. There is a bird half crying
and there are the waves half moaning, these are the sounds.
My nose alone is showing, most of my head
is buried, I should have a straw in my mouth
to breathe with and a periscope for my eye
to see the flags and see the derrick. I lie
in coldness, only my lips are burning; I crack
my blanket, I am free again, I rise
with sand on my shoulder, stomach, thighs. The calcium
ruins my arm; I try to wipe my back

and scream in pain; I crash into the water;
it is my justice there, in the blue, in the brown,
and I am happy. I find my stone with one breath
and rub the hatchings. It is a rolled-up scroll.
It is a book. I swim a few short lengths,
to Ireland and back, and end up walking the planks.
It is either the dream of Asbury Park
where it is built on clouds and there are cherubs
holding it end on end, or it is the city
itself, a state senator at one end,
a Confederate Legionnaire at the other,
in front of Perkins, with an unlined notebook,
ready for my own visionary window,
ready for a whole morning of sunlight and silence.

Hobbes

I am here again
walking through the Long Term parking,
fighting the cold.
My mind is on Hobbes,
how he would fare on the small bus,
what luggage he would carry,
what he would do with his meanness.
I climb the two steps
and with my two red eyes
I make peace with the driver.
He will drop me at Piedmont
and I will drag myself to another counter
and another nasty and brutish computer.
All is poor and selfish
sayeth the monster;
only pride and fear of death
move us.
I hold my little contract in my hand
and walk down the ramp all bloody and sovereign.
I give my number up
and lie down in my padded seat
and tie myself in.
After a while I will be warm and happy,
maybe when breakfast is being carried in,
maybe when lunch;
and though Hobbes be with me
I will sing in my seat
and fall asleep over Kansas and southern Utah.
I will wake in the dark
and put my left shoe on over one mountain
and my right shoe on over another.
When the time comes
I will put my ugly suitcase in the narrow aisle

and wait for the bodies in front of me.
He who meets me, or she,
will know me by my flower
or the lines around my eyes
or my wolf walk,
and I will be his or hers forever,
three full days or more.
I will live in the sunshine
and breathe the air
and walk up and down the brown grass
and the white cement.
I will keep the beast
in my breast pocket
or the inside of my briefcase
next to the wine stain and the torn satin.
Going back
I will reconsider all my odd connections
and prepare for that long slow descent
through Altoona and Harrisburg and Whitehouse, New Jersey,
by whispering and sighing as always.
If Hobbes is there
we will get on the Long Term bus together
and I will be his—or hers—forever,
two or three minutes or more,
at least until we reach the shelters.
I have my number in one of my twelve pockets
and he has his.
He sings, you know, in bed,
and still plays tennis,
not so bad for an Englischer.
We drift apart on Route 22
and Route 24, going west and east.

This was a lifetime friend,
although we'd be apart sometimes for years.
I know no one
who loved his own head more.
I'll tell this story:
when Charles II turned against him
he stayed in bed for seven days and nights
murdering bishops.
He wrote a complete version of the *Iliad* and the *Odyssey*
when he was ninety.
He never gave up his wild attempt
to square the circle.
I make the turn on Route 78
singing Villa-Lobos.
I am a second soprano.
Life has been good the past eight years,
the past two months.
I write a letter to myself
on force and fraud in the twentieth century.
I write a long and bitter poem
against the sovereign,
a bastard, whoremonger and true asshole,
as always, my darling.

Grapefruit

I'm eating breakfast even if it means standing
in front of the sink and tearing at the grapefruit,
even if I'm leaning over to keep the juices
away from my chest and stomach and even if a spider
is hanging from my ear and a wild flea
is crawling down my leg. My window is wavy
and dirty. There is a wavy tree outside
with pitiful leaves in front of the rusty fence
and there is a patch of useless rhubarb, the leaves
bent over, the stalks too large and bitter for eating,
and there is some lettuce and spinach too old for picking
beside the rhubarb. This is the way the saints
ate, only they dug for thistles, the feel
of thorns in the throat it was a blessing, my pity
it knows no bounds. There is a thin tomato plant
inside a rolled-up piece of wire, the worms
are already there, the birds are bored. In time
I'll stand beside the rolled-up fence with tears
of gratitude in my eyes. I'll hold a puny
pinched tomato in my open hand,
I'll hold it to my lips. Blessed art Thou,
King of tomatoes, King of grapefruit. The thistle
must have juices, there must be a trick. I hate
to say it but I'm thinking if there is a saint
in our time what will he be, and what will he eat?
I hated rhubarb, all that stringy sweetness—
a fake applesauce—I hated spinach,
always with egg and vinegar, I hated
oranges when they were quartered, that was the signal
for castor oil—aside from the peeled navel
I love the Florida cut in two. I bend
my head forward, my chin is in the air,
I hold my right hand off to the side, the pinkie

is waving; I am back again at the sink;
oh loneliness, I stand at the sink, my garden
is dry and blooming, I love my lettuce, I love
my cornflowers, the sun is doing it all,
the sun and a little dirt and a little water.
I lie on the ground out there, there is one yard
between the house and the tree; I am more calm there
looking back at this window, looking up
a little at the sky, a blue passageway
with smears of white—and gray—a bird crossing
from berm to berm, from ditch to ditch, another one,
a wild highway, a wild skyway, a flock
of little ones to make me feel gay, they fly
down the thruway, I move my eyes back and forth
to see them appear and disappear, I stretch
my neck, a kind of exercise. Ah sky,
my breakfast is over, my lunch is over, the wind
has stopped, it is the hour of deepest thought.
Now I brood, I grimace, how quickly the day goes,
how full it is of sunshine, and wind, how many
smells there are, how gorgeous is the distant
sound of dogs, and engines—Blessed art Thou,
Lord of the falling leaf, Lord of the rhubarb,
Lord of the roving cat, Lord of the cloud.
Blessed art Thou oh grapefruit King of the universe,
Blessed art Thou my sink, oh Blessed art Thou
Thou milkweed Queen of the sky, burster of seeds,
Who bringeth forth juice from the earth.

Knowledge Forwards and Backwards

This was city living in the 1930s,
making machine guns out of old inner tubes,
fighting above the garages. It was peaceful
killing and spying and maiming; sometimes we smoked
cigars, or roasted potatoes—we used gloves
to reach into the coals; sometimes I put
a cinder to my lips, a charred and filthy
piece of wood, then stirred through the fire hunting
my lost potato. We were not yet assimilated,
nothing fit us, our shoes were rotten; it takes
time to adjust to our lives, ten and twelve years
was not enough for us to be comfortable—
after a while we learn how to talk, how to cry,
what causes pain, what causes terror. Ah, we had
stars, in spite of the sulphur, and there was dreaming
as we came into the forties. I remember
the movies we went to—I am spending my life
accounting now, I am a lawyer, the one
with blood on his lips and cash in his pockets. I reach
across for the piece of paper, it is cardboard
from one blue shirt or another, there are columns,
I whistle as I study them. There is
a seal on the boardwalk, just about the size
of a tiny burro, the one I rode was blind
and circled left, the miniature golf is the same,
the daisies are there on the seventh hole, the palms
are crooked as always, the fences are rusted, the windmills
are painted blue and white, as always, the ocean
is cold, I hated the ocean, Poseidon bounced me
over and over, I was gasping then,
trying to get a breath, and I am gasping
now, my rib is broken, or bruised, the muscle
inside the bone, or over the bone. I have

a hundred things to think about, my mind
goes back, it is a kind of purse, nothing
is ever lost. I wait for the pain to change
to pleasure, after a while my lips will stop moving,
I will stop moaning, I will start sleeping, one day
there is an end, even if at this end
there is lucidity and gruesome recollection
and I am paying for every red mark and blue mark.
I have the calendar in front of me;
I have the pencil at my lips, but no one
can live in place of us, there is no beast
on the seventh hole to save us; the grass is false,
it is a kind of cellophane, it is
produced in shops, above garages, maybe
in spare bedrooms or out of car trunks; there is
no spirit with her finger on her forehead
and her mouth open; there is no voice for sobbing
so we can sob with it a little, although —
and I am only beginning to feel this — I am
accumulating — what could I call it, a shadow? —
I am becoming a kind of demon, you turn
into a demon, with knowledge forwards and backwards,
backwards, forwards, you develop a power,
you develop a look, you go for months
with sight, with cunning, I see it in older men,
older women, a few of them, you stand
at some great place, in front of the Port Authority
or facing the ocean, you see the decade in front of you,
you see yourself out there, you are a swimmer
in an old wool suit, you are an angry cabbie,
you are a jeweler, you are a whore, the smell
of burned pretzels is everywhere, you walk
backwards and forwards, there is a point where the knot

is tied, you touch your fingers, you make a cage,
you make a roof, a steeple, at last you walk
forwards and backwards, your shirt is thin, your elbows
are getting longer, you are a type of demon,
you can go forth and forth, now it's the ocean
now it's the Port Authority, now you are sixty,
standing behind the pretzel man, amazed
at the noise around you, amazed at the clothes, amazed
at the faces; now you are twelve, you stand in a little
valley of water, you study the sand, you study
the sky, it was a violent journey, you end up
forgetting yourself, you stand at some place, there are
thousands of places, you stand in the Chrysler Building
beside the elevators, you stand in a lookout
on Route 78, you stand in the wooden post office
in Ocean Grove, in front of the metal boxes;
it is a disgrace to dance there, it is shameful
snapping your fingers, if we could just be singers
we'd walk down Main Street singing, no one as yet
has done this, three and four abreast, the language
could be Armenian, it could be Mohawk—
that is a dream too, something different from Whitman
and something different from Pound. What a paradise,
in front of the Quaker Inn, the women are watching,
I'm singing tenor, someone is taking a picture.
For me, when there is no hierarchy, for me,
when there is no degradation, when the dream
when lying is the same as the dream when walking,
when nothing is lost, when I can go forth and forth,
when the chain does not break off, that is paradise.

Lyric

I wonder who has pissed here
and stared—like me—at those wild petunias
or touched a purple leaf from that small pear tree.

Has anyone lain down here
beside those red peppers
or under those weak elm withers
standing in shame there?

Dear god of that grape,
has anyone snapped off a little curlicue
to see if it's wood or wire
or stripped the bark off those thick vines
and leaned against that broken fence?

Has anyone put some old parsley in his mouth
to see what the taste is
or lifted a rose mum to his face
to see if he'll live forever?

My Favorite Farewell

There is a kind of mop hanging down from the tree.
It is a willow. It has its own sad branches
somewhere. There is a huge Greek crypt
in front of the tree and there are stairs going down
to some kind of darkness. In the other corner
there are three cypresses—they stand alone
against a light blue sky—and there are flowers
around the crypt and bushes on the hillside.

Sadness is everywhere. Hector is holding
his wife's thin wrist and staring into her eyes.
Her hand is hanging loosely on his neck
and she is holding back her tears. A plume
is sitting on his helmet and a beard
is hanging from his neck; his skirt is made
of gorgeous pelts and there are purple thongs
around his leg tied in a little ribbon.

What else? The nurse is holding the baby. He is
enormous. Andromache's robes are flowing.
There are pompoms on her shoes and disks
holding her sleeves up, and her girdle. Her hair
is wavy and hanging to her waist but the nurse's
is just below her fluted ear. Hector
is resting his right hand on a shield—it's more
like a lopsided wheel. He doesn't have a spear.

What else? There is a pond underneath the cypresses
and they are on a hill. There is an effort
at vegetation beside the pond. Hector's
sleeves are rolled up. Andromache is in motion.
The crypt is out of proportion; the background is missing
on the left side; the steps seem to go up

instead of down; there is a violet filagree
behind the steps; the pillars are covered with disks.

It is my favorite farewell. As I watch it
I know Achilles will tear off Hector's helmet
and drag his body through the dust, and I know
his enemies will spit on him and stab
him and the dogs will feed on his blood. I pay
attention to these things. It is the only
life we have. I am happy to be here
in front of the silk work and embroidery

watching them say good-bye. They will have to
make do with their sentiments and banalities.
That is all they have. Their hands are clumsy.
Their hills are unconvincing. Their clouds are muddy.
They are lucky to have the cypresses
and they are lucky that there's a streak of blue
behind the willow. I press against the glass.
There is a nail stuck inside the silk

that adds another oddness to the painting,
that makes it flat and distant and ruins illusion—
if there was any illusion—although it may
have fallen from the backing and slid down
the sky and down the shield and through the ribbons
into the dirt. I kiss the baby good-bye.
I kiss the nurse good-bye. The snow is falling
and I will be walking in the street half buried

inside my overcoat. I remember
the ending now. They put his white bones
in a golden box and wrapped it in soft purple

before they covered it up with dirt and stones.
That was a nice farewell—Andromache sobbing,
Hecuba howling, Helen tearing her hair out.
I think it is the cypresses that moved me
the most although it is the mop-faced willow

that is the center of the grief. The cypresses
are like a chorus standing on top of the sky
and moaning—they are moaning about the wind
and moaning about the narrow steps; they sit
on the edge of a hill, they hardly are planted, they whisper
about Achilles: "Think of Achilles," they whisper.
"Think of his tapered spear, think of his shield
with three kinds of metal, thicker than a wrist,

heavier than a door, think of lifting it
and holding it up with one huge hand while the other
searches the air and dances"—I find it moving
in spite of the stiffness and pallor of the figures,
in spite of the missing leg and floating branches.
It is my fondness for those souls. It is
my love of childish trees and light blue skies
and flowing robes. I have to be forgiven.

For Once

It was in southern Florida I reached
my foot across to trap a soul. He strayed
from one orange tile to another; he would live
for twenty seconds under my shoe, then run
to his door and pant an hour or two. I watched him
climb his wall. He turned his head and stared.
He lifted one gluey leg, then another.

He was from Enoch, one of the little false ones
full of mathematics and wizardry,
a slave to the moon. We yodeled and sang together—
it was like scraping chalk—I touched his throat.
It was translucent. I could see the spiders
going down his gullet. "Just one more song," I sang,
and there, two blocks from the ocean, six thousand years
into our era, we stood on the street and shouted.

There was a sunset somewhere. Someone cranked
a window open, as if to listen. Beyond that
there were our noises, an airplane droning, a car
beginning a trip, a baby screaming, a woman
yelling in Spanish. We stood beside each other—
if you could call that standing, and speculated.
We were mediators. I rubbed his head
and his yellow eyes began to close. The two of us
were getting ready for something—I could tell that—
before we lost each other.
                                    I was left
with the bougainvillaeas and the narrow sidewalk
and the chain-link fences and the creeping vines.
I kept the music secret, walking south
on the left side of the road, beside the mosses.
Our sound was southern, mixed a little with Spanish,

mixed a little with French, and Creole. For once
there was no Polish, or German. I was adjusting
to the dunes and swamps, although there was some forties,
and thirties too; the last thing I did was whistle
and ring the fences. I was alone now and wandered
up and down those streets. I thought of the tail;
I thought of the heart. I don't know about the heart,
how many chambers there are, how cold it gets,
where it shunts the blood to, what the pulse is,
if it's a *clumsy* heart, if it can love
like ours can, if it can be grown again, if food
destroys it and exercise renews it, if memory
can make it flutter, if passion can make it flow.

This I thought about going south on one street
and east on another, picking up coconuts
and holding them to my ear, tearing the fronds up
and wearing them like a shawl. It was a kind
of happiness, shrieking and hollering in the tropics,
watching my skin grow dry and my blood grow thin,
wandering through a forest of cypress roots,
finding someone that old and wise. I loved it.

Steps

There are two hundred steps between my house
and the first café. It is like climbing a ladder.
I gasp and pant as if I were pulling a mule,
as if I were carrying a load of dirt. I do
the journey twice—I left the key in the car
the first time down. There is another hill
above the first—the road to the car—another
one hundred steps. But I was born in Pittsburgh
and I know hills; I know that second rise
after a leveling off; I know the gentleness
between the two pair of steps, I know the wear
at the center, if it is stone, the soft splinters,
if it is wood, and I know the broken spaces,
the rhythm stoppers—railroad ties—but even
worse, I know the broken heights, four inches
and then a foot, and then another foot,
or fourteen inches, and the curves that carry you
around and around. There is a street on the South Side—
Pittsburgh again—that goes up hundreds of feet.
It is a stairs. I walked until my thighs
had turned to stone; and there were walkways like that
on the side of streets and cars that only made it
partway up, some turned around, some facing
the houses, abandoned cars. I am in Samos,
a village called Stavrinidhes, halfway up
the mountain of Ampelos. The town of Ampelos
is two miles away, a forty-minute walk.
I sit all day and watch. The sea is on my left.
The hills are all around me. Today is the walk
to Manolates, an hour and a half by foot,
a little less by car; it is a mulepath
up and down the ridges. I like the streets

in Ampelos. You climb for fifteen minutes,
your legs go slower and slower; this time there is
the long slope, the slant between the steps,
no relief at all, and there are two steps
twenty-five inches apiece, and there is a stairs
with a tree at the top, it is a kind of pyramid,
a kind of throne, the tree is a king, it sits there
painted white, and there is a waterfall
of steps, it almost pours. I touch a window
on my left, I touch a curtain, there is a trumpet vine
in front of the house, there is wisteria—
a limb that stretches half a block—I touch
a cactus, I touch a telephone pole, I reach
the hill above the town. The thing about climbing
is how you give up. I sit on a rock. I am
in front of a mountain. There's a white horse behind me,
there's a two-foot cypress beside me, it's already
burdened with balls. I am waiting for Hera,
she was born on this island. Zeus must have roared
on every mountain, he must have lifted a pine tree
to make a bed for them, or scooped out a valley.
Ah, Lord, she was too full of anger. The clock
says something on one side, something else on the other.
It rises above the houses. There are some towns
in Pennsylvania like this, and West Virginia;
I have sat on mountains. Imagine Zeus
in West Virginia, imagine the temple to Hera
in Vandergrift, Pa. My heart is resting,
my back feels good, my breathing is easy. I think
of all my apartments, all that climbing; I reach
for a goldenrod, I reach for a poppy, the cross
is German more than Greek, our poppies are pale

compared to these. I gave up on twenty landings,
I gave up in Paris once, it was impossible,
you reach a certain point, it is precise,
you can't go farther; sometimes it's shameful, you're in
the middle of a pair of stairs, you bow
your head, your hand is on the rail; your breath
is hardly coming; sometimes you run to the top
so you can stop at the turning, then your legs burn,
sometimes they shake, while you are leaning over
and staring down the well or holding your arm
against the wall. Sometimes the stairs are curved,
that makes a difference, sometimes the risers are high,
sometimes there are too many turns, your knees
cannot adjust in time. Sometimes it's straight up,
landing after landing. Like a pyramid.
You have to lean into the steps, you have to
kneel a little to stop from falling backwards.
I turn around to look at the mountain. There is
a little path going up, some dirt and stones;
it would take two more hours. The wind is almost
roaring here—a gentle roar—the ocean
is green at first, then purple. I can see Turkey.
Who knows that I have given up? I hear
two women talking, I hear a rooster, there is
the back of a chimney, seventy bricks, there is
a cherry tree in blossom, there is a privy,
three hundred bricks to a side, there is a cat
moaning in Greek. You would look at the cherry tree,
you would rest your feet on a piece of marble,
you would be in semi-darkness; there are
dark pink cherries on the roof, the bowl
is sitting on a massive base, the floor

is dirt, there is no door. I wave to a donkey,
I read his lips, his teeth are like mine, I walk
to the left to see the oven, I count the bricks,
I look at the clock again, I chew my flower.

V I

from

Bread Without Sugar

1 9 9 2

Three Hearts

A chicken with three hearts, that is a vanished
breed, a day of glory in the corn,
romance against a fence. It was the sunset
just above New Egypt that made me wince,
it was the hay blown up from Lakewood. God
of chance, how much I loved you in those days,
how free I felt and what a joy it was
sitting there with my book, my two knees braced
against the dashboard. How empty it was then,
and how my mind went back. How many hearts
did the chickadee have? How much whistling and singing
was in those fields? How far did I have to go
to disappear in those grasses, to pick those trillium?

The Founder

There was a kind of drooping bronze head
I stole in the Catskills and put in my living room
in Philadelphia. I put a sledge hammer
beside it so my friends and I could smash him
and change his shape from thoughtful oppressor
to tortured victim. This was just to show
the close connection between the two, the liquid
life of Capitalism; we got to kick him,
we got to gouge his eyes out, we were elated
breaking his nose and flattening his ear; it was
a kind of funeral rite, sometimes the hammer
hummed in our hands, there was a jolt, his pain
was in our wrists; sometimes we were exhausted
from so much pounding; after a while his face
was old and twisted, it was a little shameful.
I finally sold him—by the pound, I think;
he was too ugly for us, too demented;
we were starting to turn to pity—we pitied
that bronze bastard, he who must have presided
over the burning of mountains, he who managed
the killing of souls, the death of every dream.

I reached inside once to get the brain
but it was only rough casting in there,
nothing to suck on, even though the cavity
was widened at the base of the skull. He was
a brainless founder, his eyes stared at the wall,
or if we turned him around his eyes stared
with a kind of wonder at the dining-room table
catching the pools of beer. I remember
it wasn't all raw Socialism and hatred
of the rich; there was a little terror in it.
I think sometimes I got out of bed early

and put a towel or a T-shirt over his face
to cover his eyes and his ugly deformities.
He was for a while a mutilated ancestor,
someone we had buried twice, a monster,
something that could ruin us. It took an effort
to put him on the back of a station wagon
and free ourselves from fright. I had to struggle.
Although I'm sorry I sold him, he deserved
to be buried somewhere. I should have driven
to one of the dumps and thrown him into a valley
between a sofa and a refrigerator,
or just gone into the woods and made a grave
between two birches and shoved him in. I'm glad
there wasn't a river; I would have dropped him
down in the muck with the black Budweiser,
and one cold spring the current would have carried him
through a park or into a muddy backyard
on top of the poison and the wild strawberries,
or carried him into the open, his crushed head
going faster and faster, turning around in the garbage,
his face forever swollen, his eyes squinting,
the sorrow coming from his metal lips,
the sun shining down, the melodies never ending.

Nice Mountain

Great little berries in the dogwood,
great little *buds*, like purple lights
scattered through the branches, perfect wood
for burning, three great candelabra
with dozens of candles, great open space
for sun and wind, great view, the mountain
making a shadow, the river racing
behind the weeds, great willow, great shoots,
great burning heart of the fields, nice leaves
from last year's crop, nice veins and threads,
nice twigs, mostly red, some green and silky,
nice sky, nice clouds, nice bluish void.

I light my candles, I travel quickly
from twig to twig, I touch the buttons
before I light them—it is my birthday,
two hundred years—I count the buds,
they come in clusters of four and seven,
some are above me, I gather a bunch
and hold it against my neck; that is
the burning bush to my left, I pick
some flaming berries, I hang them over
my tree, nice God, nice God, the silence
is broken by the flames, the voice
is a kind of tenor—there is a note
of hysteria—I came there first,
I lit the tree myself, I made
a roaring sound, for two or three minutes
I had a hidden voice—I try
to blow the candles out, nice breath,
nice wagon wheel, great maple, great chimes,
great woodpile, great ladder, great mound of tires,
nice crimson berries, nice desert, nice mountain.

How Would It Be?

How would it be at my age to burn some land
between a Chinese willow and a white mulberry?

What would I do with the smoke
that blows first toward the television wires

and then reverses itself to curl some flowers
still hanging from the dwarf apple?

Couldn't my love be in that fire, wouldn't she
just adore those ashes, wouldn't she just love to stir

a stick in that dust, and wouldn't she love to dream
of another birth and another conversion?

Couldn't she get on her knees? Couldn't she also
smear her face with dirt? Couldn't she explode?

Grinnell, Iowa

Guy Daniels would have loved May
if he could see those teachers coming toward him
with baked chicken and white wine in their arms.
He would have bent down a little
and closed his eyes the way he did
to smell a lilac or a wet spirea.
When I drive through those empty streets or past
the giant feed stores and storage sheds
I think of how he lived in New York, the shame
of all those steps, the uncontrolled steam, the terrible
darkness of his rooms. I have heard him
rage against five administrations. I have
listened to his jokes—in French and Russian—
and I have heard him shout at three wives and anger
his few friends with his endless self-pity
but I have never heard him talk about this state
with anything but affection. When I drive
four times over the Iowa River, because
it twists underneath our highways, I half-see
Guy Daniels in 1941 just starting
a life in the East, some precious books, a few
shirts and ties, a smile on his face, a young
man's gloom and purity surrounding him
like a white cloud, the cloud of steam that goes by
his unwashed window. I half-see him changing
trains in Chicago, his suitcase is on his shoulder,
his coat is open. The war is what ruined him, Nixon
ruined him, living three years in Washington, living
by his wits in New York City, the best translator
of Russian in America; leaving Iowa,
forgetting the River Road outside Ottumwa,
forgetting the streaks of lightning over the Capitol.

Walking toward those teachers my eyes water
as if I were Guy Daniels. I half-bow
to show respect. I keep thinking it is
the second decade of the twentieth century,
or maybe as late as 1940. I bend
to pick a few spring beauties, they are scattered
like what? like snow? snow in May? They last
one hour I think; I give them to the tall
wife in the linen dress; she would have adored
me once; I can hear a cardinal; there is
nest after nest in the woods; I think of the streamliner
racing toward Cedar Falls, but I am
once removed—I am not Daniels—I think of
the stone hills in the north, the black trucks
pointed into the curb, the bitter farm
holidays, the empty corn palace.

I pick a poppy—made of paper—it is
the color of the one I buy each year
May thirtieth, or the Monday before.
I pull a caterpillar from my shirt;
I give him another home, a green leaf
surpassing all green leaves; I watch him with a straw,
a kind of supple vein I took from a leaf
the next one over to his. I keep away ants
and birds. He is half bursting with desire,
he almost is ready for his molt, he almost
is ready for his week of rage and sorrow.

Ukrainian

FOR ROBIN BEEMAN

Before I go outside I daub my face
with vinegar. That is Ukrainian. I put
one drop behind my knee and one on my earlobe.
I choose a bush. If there is a flower I scatter
a grain of sugar on the twig to help
the flying worms; I pick a weed; I prop
a rain-drenched tulip. There is a part of me
that lives forever. Spring after spring I sit
at my redwood table; at this point the grain is white
with age, the boards are splintered, the hole that held
a grand umbrella is bent, or twisted, nothing
could fit there. Yet I'm enchanted. I sit on the bench—
one of two—half-curved—the table itself
is round, it measures more than a yard, the end boards
are split and shattered. I have one favorite tree
and one favorite bird. I lift my cocoa. Water
is all around me. I make a pact; if the tree
lasts one more year, if it blooms next spring, if the flowers
that cover the twigs and fill the sky come back again
I'll stay here another winter, I'll plant a garden,
I'll trim my branches, I'll rake my leaves. The cardinal
who lives beside the redbud, he whose crimson
is richer than that pink, he who almost
shames the tulips, he whose carnal cry
is always loud and florid, he is my witness.

What It Is Like

I will have to tell you what it is like
since I was the one lying on my back
with my arms in the air and a blanket up to my
chin, since I was the one on a mattress
and the one trying to make up my mind
whether it was an early heaven just being there
or whether it was another bitter vertigo.

There were great parties where I went out
on a back porch and stared through the sycamores,
and there were parties, mostly lawless gatherings,
where we stood on the beach apart from each other
studying the sky. For me it's always
the earth; I'm one of the addicts; I can hardly
stand the dreaminess; I get burnt, I blister

at night as others do in the day. Last summer
I lay there crying. It was California
and the sheep vision. I was on a mattress
looking up. I started to talk. Aside
from the stars, aside from the beating heart, I only
remember two things: both hands were in the air
and I was, for the first time in twenty years,

lying down without fear. My friend Robin
was there beside me; she was sobbing; I have
such gratitude toward her. It was her house,
it was her stars. She took me down to see
the sheep first, then she showed me the ocean.
It was an outside room; one wall was a maple,
one wall was made of planter boxes. There were

tomatoes and eggplants in one, there was lavender
and basil in another. I remember
the trees on every side; I know there was oak
and redwood; there was a twisted madrona with leaves
in leathery piles, almost like rhododendron.
Robin knew the shadows, she knew the edges,
she knew the clouds, she knew the sky. It was

the summer of 1989. The charts
have already registered my odd affliction
and the stars absorbed my happiness. Standing—
or lying—you could see a horse to the right,
if you were facing north, and a white dragon,
if you were facing south. I think I never
slept that night. I only dozed. And ranted.

Her Right Eye Catches the Lavender

FOR JUDY ROCK

What is the eastern gull called? Is it the same one
that floats in the Iowa River? I read in *Birds*
it has pink legs—yellow eyelids in summer.
Why did I never see that? Can I drive
a thousand miles to live among them, watch
them hop and lift their wings a little, see them
fold their legs back as they soar? Someone

named Rock was walking by the water; she threw
salami at them. Knowing her as I do
I know she chose one of them and pursued him
relentlessly—her eye is part of her mind—
and though there would be patter she never would lose him
until he was gone. I don't know how she feels
about them as scavengers, I don't know if she
calls them rats with wings or if she finds them
endearing, as I do, with their gorged bodies
and drooping wings—gobbling doves—if she
forgives them, as I do, for their gluttony,
if she watches them fighting the currents, if she compares them
to hawks, if she compares them to pigeons. After

her walk on the beach she lay down with her clothes on
in one of those shingled houses, on starched sheets
with eyelets at the borders, maybe flowers—
faded peas or roses. There was a roomful
of crisp white linen, there was a pear-shaped bottle
with three carnations, there was a wedding bouquet
with ivory streamers—curled up on the bureau—
and there was a drawing of Thomas Hardy's birthplace
in Dorset, and a painting above the bed
of an apple orchard in bloom, it was cloudy
and humming. She woke up at six and watched

the light get stronger in the windows, the one
a lemon pink, the other a pearl gray,
both of them filled with branches, and she thought
a little about her happiness. Day and night

the gulls eat, although they rest; they fall
asleep in a second. Even if there is some shifting,
even gurgling, they are asleep. It is
sleep that alters their rage, sleep slows down
their appetites, it is their only substitute
for pity—even as it renews
their life of greed. I think she must get up,
I think she smiles; she rummages through her suitcase
looking for something, she kneels at the foot of the bed
with one hand under her chin; her right eye catches
the lavender. I have her letter, I am
more voracious than I was seven years ago
but I am more lenient. I watch them catch the wind,
then race downstream. Why did it take so long
for me to get lenient? What does it mean one life
only? Could I not stand in the mud
beside my black willow, thinking of her and loving her?

His Song of the Green Willow

I guide my darling under the willow tree
to increase the flow of her blood.

A branch weeps, so does she, a twig breaks off
like one of her thoughts.

We are helpless together, we spend the night
listening to shameless sounds

and study the moon together, watching it spread
knowledge over the white mulberry.

Whoever lies down first, that one will hear
the cardinal first, and that one will see the streaks

above the lilacs. Whoever does not leave,
whoever is loyal, whoever stays, that one will see

the rabbits thinking, that one will see a nest
and small ones warm from living. Whoever sits up

and looks at the sky—whoever is alone—
that one will be the griever, that one will make

his song out of nothing, that one will lean on his side
and stir the ground with his stick—and break his stick—

if that is his way, and moan, if that is his way,
and go on forever—his thirty-two feet at a time—

thirty-two feet until the branches start
and the scattered twigs,

her thoughts again—for him her thoughts—his song
of the green willow, her song of pain and severance.

I Would Call It Derangement

I cut a stick for my love. It is too early
to clear the yard. I pick some lilac. I hate them
dying on the vine. I plan my assault
on the dead maple. I will tie some rope
to the rotting side and pull it down so I can
cut it limb from limb without destroying
the phone connections from one state to another
or smashing the new tomato plants and ruining
the asters. She is walking from place to place
and wrapping herself in sheets. If the wind
were free up there it would lift the curtains
just as it bends the poppies and the yearning
iris. I am setting a table. I
am smiling at the Greeks next door. I put
an old gardenia in the center, something
that has some odor. We are in the flowery
state now. I spill half the petals over
her watermelon; only here are flowers
good for eating, here and India
where they are sprinkled over colored ice
and onto the half-cooked fish. I have a system
for counting bricks but this one day I study
the clouds that move from left to right and the swallows
hunting for food. They seem to fly in threes
and alternately flap their wings, then skim
the roofs; they even make a sound, some brief
chipping; I hear it when they come in range,
maybe when they fight for space. One cloud
is black, it goes from a simple skeleton
to a bloated continent. Given my inclination,
I will turn it into a blowfish before
breakfast is over—or an uprooted tree.
Upstairs she sings—she chips—I know she's dancing

with something or other. When she comes down she'll have
the static of the radio on her tongue,
she understands the *words*, she actually sings
those songs—her voice is a high soprano—I
love it going up and down. My voice is ruined
but I can do a kind of quaver. I have
unearthed the wisdom from my second decade,
and though it did the world little good and even
served as a backdrop to our horrors I don't
blame the music, I can't blame the music
if the horrors grow stronger every year.
She listens to me with one hand, eating sugary
pineapple with the other. I listen too,
under the washrag and the dead maple,
hearing the words for the first time, making her scream
with laughter at my words, almost lucid
compared to hers, as hers are labyrinthian
compared to mine. There is this much music
in eastern Pennsylvania and this much love
and this much decadence. I would call it
derangement—the swallows twice a day
have it, and the white delphiniums
turning to blue again and the orange snapdragons.
If we could lie down for a minute we would let
the bastardy of our two decades take over
just as we let the songs do; there is nothing
that doesn't belong with love; we can't help it
if anguish enters; even leaving the world
as we do there is no disgrace, that is
another kind of anguish—just as it was
following a band of swallows, just as it was
bending down to taste the flowers or turning
the clouds into overturned trees or smiling in Greek.

The Thought of Heaven

There is one blossom on my redwood table
I smell for hours, even holding it
like a handkerchief in the palm of my hand
and bringing it to my face. I recognize it
as a kind of thought, as in the black locust
the poor of the world for one or two weeks a year
have their paradise, nor is it disgraceful
nor is it weak and seedy even if the thorns
make their wrists bleed, even if the leaves
they love to strip are dry; as in the phlox,
the weightless phlox, the bees drag down, the six
colors of lavender, a field of wild ninnies
growing like grass where there is a little room
beside the road; as in the bridal wreath
that smells like honey, that covers a city with cream,
there is one day for pomp; as in the dogwood
there is one day for sadness, four curled petals
with drops of blood, growing white or pink
in the cold dirt, all the more to be
the contrast, under some maple or huge cherry,
for me a blossom of thought supreme, nothing
in the world like it; as in the colored weeds
on my dashboard; as in the flowers in all five pockets;
as in my blue jacket once I found twenty years
of thought—more than that—the election
of Lyndon Johnson, the death of Eleanor Roosevelt—
look how they are political—Americans
in Lebanon, in Hispaniola; I sit there
like a tailor, cleaning out lint, whatever
lint is, holding a stem in the air, rubbing
a golden flower through my fingers, catching
the spots of light. The sun is on my left,
the poppies are in my driveway, a wild exchange

is taking place in my yard, something between
my dwarf apples; yellow dust is falling
into the sweet-smelling glue—this is thought,
even if it's copulation, it is a tried
and true intrigue, an old flirtation; there are
swollen stamens and green lipstick; Plato
would be the first to forgive me, but I don't think
of forgiveness now these last few decades. I
struggle past my willow; someone has cursed me
with a weeping willow, it is Chinese and grows
in swamps best, that I remember, swamps and bogs,
that and the sycamore; if anything,
I'll turn away; if anything I'll sit
among the broken sticks facing the fenced-in
weeds, revenge on groundhogs; I will stare
for a minute or two at a private flower, that is
enough for one day—who is it wants to sit
forever anyhow? There are two months
left—I should say three—the wind and the sun
will help me, so will water, so will bees,
for all I know, and moths, and birds; ah what
dark thoughts once rested in our coats, all of us,
dogs and cats and humans, not only burrs,
not only prickles; how it scatters first
and then floats back; that is what they called
a germ; it was Hegelian; I have
to find the pre-Socratic, that is for me
what thought should be, I am a sucker still
for all of it to hang together, I want
one bundle still. When the sweet scent comes from the east,
though I call it a thought, it is, as it should be,
something that precedes thought—that is a way
of putting it—something that accompanies thought,

but it is *thought* as it drifts down over the Chinese
willow, as it floats above the table
and penetrates my doors and windows; I bow
down to it, I let it change me, that
is the purpose of thought—I call it all thought, whatever
changes you. Dear apple, I am ready.
What is it for you, is it dreaming, does that set you
free? I call a bursting "dreaming," I call
a rage and sundering by its sweet-smelling name,
as if I were a child domesticating
everything within a mile for purposes
of my own rage. There is a thought. It is
if not in this blossom then in another,
in the lilies of our highways, in the great
round thistles beside them, in the black-eyed Susan,
the flower I always bend down for, most of all—
for two or three weeks at least—in the chicory,
blue with the dust of the universe, a blue
more like lavender—I would call it purple
if I were extreme—I would say the edges
are white from gripping the sky, or they are drained
from so much thought. I call it the thought of heaven,
not too disgraceful for the chicory,
solemn and blue as it is, such is my thinking.

VII

from

Odd Mercy

1 9 9 5

Odd Mercy

I kick a piece of leather; except for the claw
it's mostly sky. Let the silkweed bury it
and let the silkweed bury the silkweed. There isn't
a particle of life there, that's if leather
can have a life. Silkweed sends its seed
to cover the body—there is grease; there are
feathers on the claw. Juice, I think,
juice of the cat, juice of the silkweed. The pods
are empty, there is no cream, only a little
white left over, dry and fluffy. Let the
nail bury the nail, let the helmet
of someone named Knute bury the helmet of someone
named Si or Cyrus. Inside the bliss is gone,
the mind is empty; it has moved from one form
of grasping to another. I lift it up,
it is a kind of football, something between
a dry tongue and a ball. I execute
a perfect dropkick, claw after claw—there still
are dropkicks in Pennsylvania. It could be
the self growing more aloof that gives me the courage,
something I can hide behind. I still
freeze when I see a corpse, the spiteful dead
imitating the living, still lying there
with a hand between their thighs, or a paw lifted up
against the light. Let the clogged-up neck
bury the clogged-up neck, let the wristbone
bury the wristbone. If there is someone named Si
let there be someone named Cyrus, let him run
like Knute ran. In my thirteenth and fourteenth year
I spent my afternoons at the Schenley Oval
running until it got dark. I was alone
on the ancient track.—Was it a mile and a quarter?—
I know the empty stands were still intact

the way they were when horses rounded the bend.
The palings were even intact. Let the dark boy
with the long face come and stand at the railing, let him
comb his hair, the part on the left, let him
wipe away the sweat, then look at the moon
while he waits for his father; he will spend his lifetime
waiting. If there is a brown seed on his shoulder,
if it came from the plant beside the fence, it is almost
lighter than life and came by air to land
as the current decided. He reaches for a twig
and breaks it off, the pods are perfect, they are
like round canoes with graceful prows and ribbing
that holds the silk together. He had vertigo—
from running, he thought—sometimes he stopped on a sidewalk
or under a tree to feel it—it was the pleasure
he kept to himself. I still have that pleasure. Who is
the football, he or I? Who is the cat?
Am I or he? The "son of man," what is that
in the other writing? He has neither a Sears
nor a Posturepedic. Let me be the father
and bury myself. Follow me. We are
sitting on wooden boxes. We are singing
without lungs! Let the sea horse bury
the sea horse, let him die standing up. The foxes
have condominiums, the birds have silkweed
but my poor son doesn't have a sofa, he
and I are snoring, don't tell a soul. I can't
at my age start a second life, where will I
find another wife—at the airport?—how can I
stand in line for a job, how can I fight
for air again, what if I had to buy
new furniture? There is a cat inside. I love him
for dying. There is a way of kicking a suitcase

in front of the agents, one foot back and onto
the scale, there are tags all over, there are
books inside and underwear, the cat
is in a rage, there is silkweed, it drifts
like insulation over the brushes, it falls
like snow in the farthest pockets, there is toothpaste
and Neutrogena and Solex; there is a clock,
I bought in Siena, it is a German clock,
a *Peter*, with three stars and a kind of forties'
face; it ticks like an ancient bomb, the size
is perfect, the paint is a little chipped, it is
a second heart for the cat and after a day
of odd mercy another one for me.

Blue

What I was hunting for was a skeleton key
and an old pack of Luckies wrapped in foil so I
could add to my silver ball. The blue that lasted
lasted for years; in fact the sky at the end
was almost stark, there was no wind, and the clouds
were puffs at the most and in a sort of childish
formation. I did this before, I walked through a mountain,
I climbed some stairs, but this time there was no letup,
I couldn't walk over the brooms, I couldn't get either
under or over a fallen tree, and salt water
almost made me blind. I wanted to match
the blues, it was that simple, I had a kind of
larkspur love. You understand that blue,
even if dark, was my connection; I would have
sworn, if someone asked me, that my blue
was like the other one and all my bitterness
was just the result of some stray degradation,
brooms in this case, a knife or two. Can I mention
my ear was pink? Can I talk about that pink?
But can I say that it was huge and spread
from ear to ear? But can I say it listened
to everything? It was pink and listened
to everything. Though I only needed one cloud
to hide behind, one puff. One puff lifted me—
it sort of sucked me in—and though my leg was
exposed the cloud concealed me. White was my face
and then some, fog was my forest, smoke was all
around me. There I was holding my dress up
with one hand, banging through the roof with the other.
Green was my rotten liver. Blue were my bloodshot eyes.

Hinglish

"Sacre Dieu," I said for the very first time
in my adult life and leaned on a tuft of grass
in the neighborhood of one green daffodil
and one light violet, and one half-drooping bluebell.

I did a stomp around my willow, driving
the cold indoors and letting the first true heat
go through my skin and burn my frozen liver.

I placed the tip of my tongue against my teeth
and listened to a cardinal; I needed at least
one more month to stretch my neck and one
for delayed heartbeats and one for delayed sorrows.

"Speak French," she said, and dove
into the redbud. "Embrassez-moi," I said.
"Love me a little," "I am waiting for the hollyhock
and the summer lily," she said. "I am waiting
to match our reds. Baisez-moi," she said,
and raced for the alley. "Here is a lily, my darling,
oranger than your heart, with stripes to match
and darker inside than you." "Parle Français,
mon cher; pick me a rose; gather roses
while ye may; lorsque tu peux." "Have you
read Tristan Tsara?" I said. "Suivez-moi,
there is a bee," she said. "Forget your mother,
Oubliez vos fils vos mères." Her voice
is like a whistle; we used to say, "what cheer,"
and "birdy, birdy, birdy." There is a look
of fierceness to her. She flies into the redbud
without hesitation. It's easier that way. She settles,
the way a bird does on a branch; I think

they rock a little. "Nettles are nettles," she says,
"fate is full of them." "Speaka English," I say

and wait for summer,
a man nothing left of him but dust
beside his redbud
a bird nothing left of her but rage
waiting for her sunflower seed
at the glass feeder.

"A single tear," I say.
"My tear is the sky you see it," she says. She has
the last word. Halways. A bird is like that. She drops
into the hemlocks. Her nest is there. It is
a thicket at the side of the house. "I hate
the bluejay," she says. In Hinglish. She flies to the alley
and back to the street without much effort though my yard
is long as yards go now. How hot it will be
all summer. "Have you read Éluard?" she says.
"He avoided open spaces; his poems
were like my bushes and hedges; there in the middle
of all that green a splash of red; do you like
'splash of red'? His instrument was the wind.
So is someone's else." She has a flutelike
descending song; when she speaks French the sky
turns blue. "On sand and on sorrow," he said. "He talks
just like you. He had a small desert too;
he had an early regret. There is a piece
of willow. I am building something. I'll speak
Hinglish now. I love simplicity.
I hate rank." "Little wing of the morning," I say.
"In the warm isles of the heart," says she.

"I hold the tenderness of the night," say I,
"Too late for a kiss between the breasts," say she.

Sitting on my porch,
counting uprights, including the ones on my left
beside the hammock, including the ones on my right
beside the hemlock,
reading Max Jacob,
speakin' a Hinglish.

Ida

Well, I am like a palm tree,
the plant of pure ugliness,
somewhere in a front yard
spared by the last hurricane,
one of the royal ones
whose glory is turned to scum,
whose riches are turned to rubbish.
It is as if its skin
was chiseled, it is as if
its hair was ripped from its head,
its dirty squirreltail fronds
turning brown on the sidewalk.
It is as if the wind
was showing it some kind of love,
the light beams of Plotinus
straight from the stars, like arrows
pointing down, like eyeballs
pointed up, the arrows
of our desire more broken,
more curved, the music coming
in English as well as Italian,
Pavarotti singing "Wien, Wien,"
my mother on the edge of her bed
staring at the lighted box,
her throat not yet closed up,
her own eyes wet with song,
a fixed smile on her lips,
her longing for the past so keen
it breathed in her, the moon
now gone from her life, the light
on the bay now gone, the Florida
of anger and melancholy
also gone, Pavarotti,

a fat angel with a beard
dressed in a silk tuxedo
with a handkerchief in his hand
singing and singing, and she,
poor Ida, poor Ida, still sitting
and smiling; it is as if
there was a kindness, as if
there was a thought to her pain,
as if the scarves in her dresser
could save her, or even the letters,
as if the bird-of-paradise
I sent her was not a simulacrum,
its yellow crown vibrating
on a true head, its blue beak
thinking, as if it prayed
the way a bird does that's shaped
like a gaudy plant—"Oh palm tree,
look at me shaking my head,
look at the red and green
flash in, flash out, may your eyes
be open to our distress,
we have polluted your name,
we have acted corruptly,
Thou art truly just—"
made of threads, you know,
a kind of netting, the flesh
is more than flesh, I hate it
because it expands by cracking,
because it grows in segments
and bends half over, because
of the swelling in the middle,
because the dead leaves envelop
the trunk, because it is home

to a thousand insects, it is
a kind of forest, because
the old skin is like burlap,
because I can't breathe, because
we sweat in Florida, because
Pavarotti and his handkerchief
are drenched, because my mother
is moving her lips—you know
how it is, the small birds drop in
and out, they stab at each other,
an airplane is booming, an ambulance
is passing by; she was
afraid of dogs, what would she
do in this swamp? The fruitwood
she loved is swollen, the wormholes
were painted on, the sun
ruined every surface, the green rug
is stiff and pale, the metal
is rusty, the lampshades are gone.
She lived here twenty-seven years,
Ida of the plain song,
Ida of Sigmund Romberg,
Ida of the Strausses,
Ida and her Henry,
Ida and her Jimmy,
Ida and her Harry,
Ida standing at the rail
of *The Song of Norway*, her hat
about to blow off, or standing
in front of St. Marks, the pigeons
eating at her heart, or Ida
dressed like Lillian Russell
the last night out in a harbor

in Venezuela or watching
La Bohème at the Nixon
in downtown Pittsburgh and eating
afterwards at Buon Giovanni's
or reading *Anna Karenina*
on the back porch on Vine Street,
her father smiling, the blue-eyed
distant saint, St. Beryl
the chicken killer, the scholar,
my secret and sorrowful mother.

Small Sunflowers

FOR KATHLEEN PEIRCE

I never saw three disks like that
   facing in all directions.
It was enough to make me think three winds
   were all there were,
and I loved the leaves that fed them. I stayed with them
   through thick and thin,
until the seeds themselves turned black and died,
   until their necks were broken
and half their faces were rubber and half were cotton.
   But first the gold dust fell
and they who prayed like any others, no they
   who almost knelt down,
whose shoulders were always bent, they gave the blessing.
   And such it always was,
the poor give to the poor. But in this case
   I saw millionaires
showering in that gold, one kind and another,
   from generals to bishops;
or our kind, whatever it is, even the young,
   those very little ones
who never earned what they spent and therefore were ignorant
   of what the sorrow is
and what the greed could come to. They must have prayed
   for mercy, that comes to me first,
and after that for wisdom, such huge flowers
   must pray for wisdom, not
for money, not for a job, or a prize, and not for
   their own yellow dust, they hardly
knew their own, there were so many, they prayed
   for everyone's dust, not one of them
was rude, not one was greedy, none of them
   rolled his eyes, none of them moaned,

or rocked his body, although it is not bad
    to do it a little. I live
in water as they do and I have gone as they do
    from place to place, although
I don't get ruined as they so quickly, I am not
    dry and broken, my leaves
aren't curled and lifeless, my crown isn't bent half over,
    my face isn't green, my petals
don't hang in the wind and fall like uprooted hair
    nor do I float in filth, but I
am sickened by lying and I am at last disgusted
    by the same corruption as they are
and I am frightened by the same destruction.
    The friend who gave them to me,
she was leaving, she was uprooted, and this
    was a way for her to stay here
and leave a trail, or surprise me or give me
    something new to go with
the dead honeycomb beside my bed. I hope
    the peaches are good there. I hope
she won't be vexed as long as I was.

The Jew and the Rooster Are One

After fighting with his dead brothers and his dead sisters
he chose to paint the dead rooster of his youth,
thinking God wouldn't mind a rooster, would he?—or thinking
a rooster would look good in a green armchair
with flecks of blood on his breast and thighs, his wings
resting a little, their delicate bones exposed, a
few of the plumes in blue against the yellow
naked body, all of *those* feathers plucked
as if by a learned butcher, and yet the head
hanging down, the comb disgraced, the mouth
open as if for screaming, the right front chair leg,
seen from a certain angle, either a weapon
or a strong right arm, a screaming arm, the arm
of an agitator; and yet at the same time the chair
as debonair as any, the brown mahogany
polished, the carving nineteenth century, the velvet
green, an old velour, as if to match
the plumes a little, a blue with a green. No rabbi
was present, this he knew, and no dead butcher
had ever been there with his burnished knife
and his bucket of sand; this was the angry rooster
that strutted from one small house to another, that scratched
among the rhubarb, he is the one who stopped
as if he were thinking, he is upside down now
and plucked. It looks as if his eye can hardly
contain that much of sorrow, as if it wanted
to disappear, and it looks as if his legs
were almost helpless, and though his body was huge
compared to the armchair, it was only more
horrible that way, and though his wings were lifted
it wasn't for soaring, it was more for bedragglement
and degradation. Whatever else there was
of memory there had to be revenge there,

even revenge on himself, for he had to be
the rooster, though that was easy, he was the armchair
too, and he was the butcher, it was a way
to understand, there couldn't be another, he had to
paint like that, he had to scrape the skin
and put the blotches on, and though it was
grotesque to put a dead rooster in an armchair
his table could have been full, or he just liked
the arrangement, or he was good at painting a chair
and it was done first—although I doubt it—or someone
brought him the bird—a kind of gift—for food was
cheap then, and roosters were easy to cook; but it was
more than anything else a kind of Tartar,
a kind of Jew, he was painting, something
that moved from Asia to Europe, something furious,
ill and dreamy, something that stood in the mud
beside a large wooden building and stared at a cloud,
it was so deep in thought, and it had tears
in a way, there was no getting around that kind
of thinking even if he stood in the middle of the room
holding his paintbrush like a thumb at arm's length
closing one of his eyes he still was standing
in the mud shrieking, he still was dying for corn,
he still was golden underneath his feathers
with freckles of blood, for he was a ripped-open Jew,
and organs all on show, the gizzard, the liver,
for he was a bleeding Tartar, and he was a Frenchman
dying on the way to Paris and he was
tethered to a table, he was slaughtered.

Fleur

FOR LARAINE CARMICHAEL

No sense lying—my own two rows of pompoms
are still alive, even in November, the frost
of October 12th meant nothing. Here I am
watching marigolds, in the dark. Can you
believe it? What do you think they looked like? Why
was I denied those little buttons, those small
orange clusters? These are like trees, and branch and divide,
they cover my daisies, they ruin my iris, there is
a forest here! How can I scoop the dirt up
with my own nails and rend my hair? There isn't
a single thing here for me to love, I feel
belittled. Where are the leaves? How can these flowers
live without leaves? It could have been the snapdragon
with swollen blossoms and dark spots in the throat,
it could have even been the daisy, Lord they
grow to supernatural heights, but there is
wisdom somewhere. I could have walked through daisies
sucking my cheeks. I could have lain like a swan
with eyelashes intact and pulled the *fleurs*—
they are called *fleurs*—she loved me all that morning,
she loved me not, she hates me, she despises me,
she was my lily, she is, or was, my lavender,
she was my delphinium, short and blue. I count
my *fleurs*, I have a way to go. I see me
walking the borders, my hands are in my pockets,
the railroad ties are *planks*, I turn to the left,
I am ready at any minute to plunge
into the marigolds and rub my hair
with maroon *fleurs*; or I am ready to cut
one or two branches and bring them inside. I have
a bucket of orange and yellow. I add some honey
and marjoram and bitters, I can rinse
my face when I want to, say all winter, and I can

start next time with *flats*, some Crown of Gold
for early rising, some Yellow Cupid for roaring,
and bury whatever is left out there, three stalks
with curled dried-up leaves, and heads bent down
like rubber mops and one small dragon, its throat
painted scarlet and three or four ox-eyed giants
with *fleurs* like impoverished nails, like filed teeth,
hanging on, I guess, to love, she loves me,
she loves my crumbling leaves, she loves my spikes,
she loves my broken stalks, she loves my mop,
and I love hers though mostly I love the light
that comes from her—her *emanation*—did I
ever think I'd say that?—and the coneflower
that rotted for two or three weeks—I loved that—
and how my fate was sealed by which direction
the stem would fall and whether the head would drop
before the leaves, and how she knew it, my *fleur.*

St. Mark's

Still like a child, isn't it?
Climbing up an iron staircase,
arguing with some Igor
over the broken lock,
letting my head hang into the sink,
rinsing my neck with cold water.

Like a wolf, wasn't it?
Or a dove that will never die.
Reading Propertius, trampling
the highest stars,
forcing my hands together,
touching the row of snow-capped garbage cans.

Swaybacked, wasn't it?
Dragging my wet feet
from one park to the other.
"Softened by time's consummate plash,"
isn't it?
Tulip of the pink forest.
Red and yellow swollen rainwashed tulip.

Most of My Life

A squirrel eating her way in and a mother cardinal
with such an eye she knew two things at once
in what was work for her lower than me here
I'm sure as close to her nest as she would allow
without engaging her whole prudent being, and I
saying cheer to her, what cheer, what cheer,
breathing my own prudent last if that was necessary,
my heart going out to her, for all she knew
my feet like bird's feet—I could be her child,
if it were necessary, and die on a thorn
or wear a dress for her and sparkle as rain does
and wear my sparkling beads and wear a sparkling
tear on my cheek or I could be as still
as she wants, I could be a stone, till her eye
is satisfied, she is so rough in these things,
she is so sloppy, look at her straw, she is
so close to my mother—is that Ida, her eye
shrewd and watching? Daughter of lilac, wife
of honeysuckle and privet—ah she has worked
and her heart is beating, she is a nurse, and a scholar,
and an architect, her slur and her rocking body
proof positive; she lands on my impatiens,
she flies to my birch, and I lie dead in her lap
and dead in the bark and dead in the grass stems, my arms
hanging out of the nest, leaves on my chest,
weeds and rootlets here and there, my stomach
a little red already and a little brown,
a twig in my mouth, but only by accident,
for there is more love than not, and she is reaching
to get the twig and I am holding on,
which is enough for one day, pity alone
enough for the two of us though there was grief

and duty too. I would have held up a lily
for her for she is not to blame; I would have
dried her tears. I did it for most of my life.

Oracle

I have a blue chair; there is a blue rock
and a weed in flower just before the hill
begins in earnest. There is a little chorus
somewhere down there and something that lost its voice
a half a century ago is starting up
again; it was a tenor, it was a boy
soprano, it lives by itself, it is
disincarnate, it moves from C to C,
and it is in a valley beside some mint,
against a cherry. I sang my heart out. I learned
to pipe early, I held my arms out, I buried
one hand in another—so we could have something
to do with our wrists, so we could expand our lungs
at the same time, so we could warble, so we could last
forever. Consider the basso profundo that sang
as if he were a string, his voice expanded
and shook, consider the alto. The hair on my face,
the hormones in my heart, the flesh in my hand—
this is how a soprano just disappeared
and a hoarse baritone with a narrow range
suddenly took her place. The sun in the desert
going quickly down, the dark from nowhere, voices
droning, voices shrieking, I am grateful.

VIII

from

New Poems

1 9 9 7

This Time

That was his picnic table and those were his two
spruce trees growing so vertical you'd think
there was some desperation, say a roof
eating the light up, say a chimney, and those
two things that flew from gutter to gutter and perched
for only a second — each of them — were the black-streaked
white-faced goblins coming to eat and sing
above the noise of cardinals and the humming
of rubber and its echoes and the roaring
of the early train. Lord, he was here again
not far from the jungle gym beside the plastic
zebra. Lord, he would stare at the lightbulb
in front of the voltage box bolted to the untarred
telephone pole. He would study the guy wire
and how it stretched between the roses, the wire
that caught the earth just so that nothing fell there
and dip his face to suck his tea without
using his hands this time and say his *chanson*
in English and French the way they did six centuries
ago without one word of rage, with reference
to the lark this time and the white hawthorne, beating
one hand and one heavy knuckle, his tongue whacking
the roof of his mouth, his musical thumb scraping
across the dining-room table, his pitiful slurs
in front of his metal quail, his fripperies
over his wooden-faced carp, his hapless rib cage
and nerveless fingers, his clumsy flutters
and three or four poor staccatos, hard time this time.

Self-Portrait in His Sixties

Going wild in the batik shop
he traced the pink fishes with his one free finger
and swam through a blossoming sea.

He startled two half-dressed women
trying on silk and cotton,
shocked and flustered that he was still there.

All his life he loved to sit in an armchair
while those he loved walked back and forth
in their wool coats or their linen blouses

and if there was a mirror he slouched a little
with his thoughtful hand under his chin
so he could watch the two reflections at the same time.

Behind the fishes, upside down, in rayon,
there was a starfish, him of course, railing
against the oysters, a starfish going wild. He put

a blue bandanna on his head, the end of
a bolt of silk, a field of daisies; he dragged
the bolt of silk from room to room, but he

wasn't laughing when he brought it back. It was
for almost a second, a *shawl*, and he, the starfish,
half-bowed before he kissed it and put it in place,

apologizing a little to the daisies
in their unending rows, especially
the white leaves, especially the blue wayside.

December 1, 1994

I put the pyracantha in a blue vase
and spread the coneflower over my kitchen table.
I had to make sure they could bear the noise
and catch the benefits of my small radio
as if they were more than flowers—glass frogs at least,
or metal quail, their ears amazed, their small heads
nodding with the music. As far as the changes
in government, as far as *that* noise, the frog
presides over that, he is a kind of congressman
anyhow with his huge mouth open to catch
the flies and beetles; he has turned green from money
sticking to his skin. As far as the coneflower,
as far as the rays, they were already gone
and only the wood was left, only the naked
beautiful heads. As far as my love was concerned
I picked them before the snow came, before the ice
filled up the cavities and the cold leaves
turned thin and curled themselves around the stem.
As far as the pyracantha, as far as the vase,
as far as the metal quail, their eyes turned up,
their tiny beaks in the air, I turned the knob
from music to religion and let it rest
on wisdom, two or three voices, an English, a German,
discussing rape in Asia, discussing starvation, the
quail nodded, even the pyracantha nodded,
and I, a little furious, I turned to Canada
to see what the French were doing. That day I ate
soba, with parsley; I ate standing up; I fed
the quail; I fed the plants, though they were dead,
I listened to the forecast, I shaved in the dark,
making sure I got both cheeks and the hair
above the bullet. Afterwards I opened
a 1970 *New York Times*, something

about the new mayor, something about a murder
behind a bush, something about a dump
on fire, either a bomb or a match, a heartless
speech by a Georgia senator, a horoscope,
a kidnapping, a stock decline. I sang
first to the cloves but I whispered to the garlic
and ate two pounds of grapes. The frog lay down,
as far as I know, with the pyracantha, it was
something like bestiality, the coneflower
wrapped itself around the vase and I
lay down on the sofa; but first I put my glasses
in my right shoe and dropped my keys in the delicate
acorn bowl, then turned my leg so the wallet
wouldn't cut my buttocks. As I recall I thought of
the quail before I went to sleep, one of them
is tall and straight, he is the watchdog, the other
bends down to eat. I have to lie just so
with my head like that and my feet like that, it is
a little small for a bed, although my sleep,
of all my happy sleeps, is happiest there
on that white silk. I had a word with the frog
and one with the pyracantha, I had to school them
considering the date; all the holidays
were happening at once and it would be
disaster if they didn't get ready. "America
may not have room for you," I said. We giggled
and turned the lights out; even a little light
can ruin your sleep, no matter how much Mozart
flows over you, no matter how much Fats Waller.
Darkness is what we love. "Darkness, darkness,"
they sang; the frog was a tenor—what a shock!—
the pyracantha was a pipe, the coneflower
a wheeze or two. I was an alto—after

all those years a measly alto with only
a little range: "Oh put us all to sleep,
it's 1994, put us to sleep,
darkness, darkness!" A little tin shout from the lower
two registers, a little rusty gasp from the upper.

Both of Them Were Sixty-Five

Ordinarily I wouldn't be introducing Aaron Copland to Ida Stern
nor be there to watch him bow ever so slightly
and appreciate her beauty—in spite of things—and see
him take in her white powder and her heavy rouge,

nor see her in her girlish role, a little bit
haughty, maybe a little flirtatious, her wisdom
something else from what I knew, a kind of
pact between them—in spite of things—and during

the second part I wouldn't have half leaned back
in those rocking theater chairs and smiled my smile
as I did then at my newly discovered mother
nor listen, as it were, almost for the first time

to his pure sounds, and watch her listen, and smile
her victory smile—in spite of things—nor see them
pass beside each other and see him bow
again, so skinny beside her, he who wore

white knickers in 1925 and gray
ribbed socks. If he were in Pittsburgh in 1920
they could have danced together after the basketball
and eaten later at Don Giovanni's and talked

for an hour or two on Vine Street, Beryl listening
with one eye open, a blue, and made some plan—
in spite of things—for another Friday or Saturday,
and he would have smiled at her music, though most respectfully,

especially the Caruso, and even listen
to the voice and the window rattling, one of my fathers
certainly, though Ida is dead, and Copland
never taught me stickball and never painted

quarter notes and eighth notes inside my crib
and never walked with her down Fifth Avenue
and through the arcade on Liberty and never
rented a room at the Roosevelt as I did

in 1948 and carry bricks
inside a suitcase for the room clerk's sake. I
was thirty-nine when they met and I was starting
to spread my gloom; she was, with her powder

and her perfume, hanging onto the nearer side,
as I am now. There would be a Greek ship captain,
a financier, a Turkish Jew, and a loving
hillbilly she met at the Moose, but none

would be like him—in spite of things—nor would there
be a spring like that one was, a bursting
you can't imagine, a marriage canopy shaking,
a fiddle to match, a fire—and candles—burning.

Swan Legs

Just for a second, when Mao stood up and walked
out of the theater in Leningrad the swan
stopped dancing and Khruschev just shrugged his shoulders
and lowered his eyes. Mao's hatred of tutus
prevailed as his hatred of Russian food
and his hatred of clean napkins. Nixon and Kissinger
sat for the swan in Washington—they passed
notes between them and when they were finished reading
they tore them in tiny pieces. The swan believed
in suffering so she floated across the stage,
well, sort of floated, and so it goes; the pricks
down there in their seats they couldn't care less, they feasted
on swan legs, they took care of themselves,
yet why should I pick on them, there is enough
feasting even without them. I usually know
pricks, the swan is lucky for such a bird
to do what she does to music, to do it to *song*,
her head in the air, so misunderstood and hated,
so wrongly loved; first her dark beak swaying,
and that is the violin, and then her leaping,
and that is the harp, or the comb—look at me forgetting
the comb, and the sweet potato, when I was a swan
myself, and I almost floated; the one I remember
she sang and trilled a little, that was a swan
with a voice, the thigh is wider than a chicken's,
the flesh is dark and stringy; it was vinegar
they forced down the throat, plain distilled white vinegar,
to soften the wild flesh and kill the suffering.

Eggshell

FOR LARRY LEVIS, 1946–1996

The color of life is an almost pale white robin's green
that once was bluer when it was in the nest,
before the jay deranged the straw and warm flesh
was in the shell. I found it while doing my forty-five
minute walk between two doors beside some
bushes and flowers. I put it in one of my pockets
keeping some space around it to protect
the pale green, an idiot carrying a dead
child inside him, something that might have broken out
anyway, a blue afterbirth shoved out of the
nest. I laid my dead like eggs on the table,
twelve tombstones to a box. I buried
dread that way, my telephone calls and letters,
and on the way I walked into a side yard
and straightened a brick—for it was May—and chased
a garter snake into his rainspout; and since it was morning
and it was hot already I put the eggshell
under a leather chair and thought of our trip
to New Orleans and used the end of a broom
to prop up a rosebush, the way we do, sweet Larry.

The Sounds of Wagner

You could call him a lachrymose animal
lying on his glasses at two in the morning
remembering the photograph of himself ice-skating
on his uncle's farm or eating hot sausages
and buttermilk or making a speech for Stevenson
on Chestnut Street in Philadelphia or talking
to Auden about Velveeta cheese or standing
for an hour in front of the Beacon Pharmacy
and pitching pennies or climbing all day long
above the Liberty Tunnel or swimming by himself
around the Steel Pier in his wool bathing suit.

He loved lavender more than anything else
and never forgot the sunsuit he wore, nor did he
ever forget looking into the tiny window
of a music listening room and seeing his darling
fucking someone else on the carpeted floor,
her earphones still intact though his—her lover's—
an Air Corps Cadet—his hung askew and the sounds
of Wagner floated or scattered throughout the room,
and he could hear it, nor did he ever forget
his walk that day through the park and how ashamed
he felt, and bitter, and how he weathered it.

Memoir

I already said we put each other's eyes out
above the garages and we crawled down the catwalks
behind the apartments to look at our parents undressing
and bathing and fucking. We pissed on the weaklings, we stood
in a circle pissing, we fucked the maids, we got
in line to take our turn, we hid in the bushes
waiting, a block away from Schenley Park, we
fought the Hunkies with homemade blackjacks, I was
already a general, I made inflammatory speeches,
and once, with three other cripples—it was World
War II and we were cripples—I threw bottles
and bricks and dirt into the windows of
our enemy's little dark stores; and as for schooling
the closest we got to our books was when we covered them
with Kraft paper every September but I had
a girlfriend who played the harp and she was thin
and wise and I was stupid with her; and forty
years later I was hosting a brunch in an elegant
downtown hotel with my wife and my teenage children
and aging mother and aging aunt and aging
friend of my mother's tortured with arthritis and there
was that girlfriend playing the harp again on a small
stage beside the tables and we stared
and exchanged numbers but I was still married and she
was changing her life again after spending thirty
years with an angry urologist; her eyes
were wet and joyous, large and trusting, out of a
drugstore novel, I was stricken, I walked for
years with that, my life was hell, the moon
never forgave me once; I love the harp
above all things, I love the lifelong vibrations,
what the world was doing, how I exploded.

Oskar

You know, the squirrel was made for me and not me for
the squirrel, and it is running up and down that causes
the turmoil, while I am sitting with my own acorn in my
mouth and, unlike him, I am ashamed of burying my money—
though I did it for my children and in the long cold night
we will pass sweet figs between us and chunks of chicken
cooked in raisin juice and carrots almost white
from so much sugar. He keeps talking about the same tree
over and over, he is relentless, and dark whiffs of
joy called knowledge or memory keep bringing him
back although only a dozen soft balls are still hanging
from one tree and truly nothing but a dried-up leaf
from the other. I warn him against the overbite
and the new dentists filling him with gold, considering
the bankers as thieves, grave robbers and protocol
keepers, but he just stalks and flounces, and he just croons,
as if he were made of water or as if he just lived
for the wheel and its aftermath. I think we may be
celebrating in different ways and even have a different
view of the slow-moving sun itself, but nonetheless
I adjust his tail and rub his stomach and kiss him
the way I did when he lived on that rough little branch
and ask his forgiveness for selling him for a dollar.

Something for Me

The tree that leaned against the side of the house
and planted leafy stringers in the gutter,
she was so ugly only because there was no
room for branches lower down and no one
could love her, either her bark or her crooked trunk;
but I have a little grief for her somewhere
between the guilty and the foolish driving
north on Route 75 between the cities of
Cincinnati and Dayton listening to
one cry after another, mostly among
the suffering and the hopeful, mostly silent,
sometimes slapping the steering wheel, deciding
too late to plant another tree near where
I cut that down, between the garbage cans
and the frozen mop—last time I looked—a dogwood
maybe, except there's not enough sun, another
green hemlock maybe—and something for me—between
the light and the weighty, something cement, a frog
or a large gray crow, with running water, although
a flower would do, something with fragrance, a lilac—
why do less?—or something early, spikenard
or Greek roses, or a blue inkwell
with a poem rolled up inside. Donkey, pass by!

Personal

I am a moth of sorts the way I strip down
leaves, and if there is a rustling sound I listen
and even ask directions since I have no fear
of being found unmanly. I even stay
sometimes to gossip with the branches about
the flowers we hate, and Mexican cooking, and lights
strung through the trees, and that always leads to Christmas
and that leads to a discussion of Christ and by some
fluke I don't understand that leads to welfare
and gun control and Madison's viewpoint and how many
guns the average New Mexican owns and the average
New Yorker, counting the Projects and counting the gated
communities and whether your Lord would like it
walking on carpets, or call it my Lord, and who
would wash whose feet and whether his name is Jesus
or Joshua and if his hair was red and who
gave whom the vinegar and what did I sing.

Lilacs for Ginsberg

I was most interested in what they looked like dead
and I could learn to love them so I waited
for three or four days until the brown set in
and there was a certain reverse curl to the leaf by
which in putting my finger on the main artery
beside the throat I knew the blood had passed on
to someplace else and he was talking to two
demons from the afterlife although it was
just like the mountains in New York State since there was
smoke in the sky and they were yelping and he was
speaking in his telltale New Jersey English
and saying the same thing over and over the way he
did when he was on stage and his white shirt was
perfect and the lack of air and of light
aged the lilacs but he was sitting on a lily
in one or two seconds and he forgot about Eighth Street
and fame and cancer and bent down to pick a loose
diamond but more important than that he talked
to the demons in French and sang with his tinny voice
nor did he go on about his yellowing sickness
but counted the clusters and said they were only stars
and there were two universes intertwined, the
white and the purple, or they were just crumbs or specks
that he could sprinkle on his pie nor could he
exactly remember his sorrow except when he pressed
the lilacs to his face or when he stooped
to bury himself in the bush, then for a moment
he almost did, for lilacs clear the mind
and all the elaborations are possible in their
dear smell and even his death which was so
good and thoughtful became, for a moment, sorrowful.

Shad

FOR JOANNE BUZZETTA

Sometimes he reached for a blood orange
so he could feel the stickiness of everyday life,
as if he needed something beside the dormant buttonwood
balls outside his wavy window or the
sky turning blue in the center of his uprooted city.

And sometimes he cursed the mayor for tearing down
the fish market and planting harsh yellow lights
on the two streets leading into and out of the square.

When he smoked a cigar it was either a Marsh
Wheeling or a Parodi, the one in memory of
his grandfather Jacob who owned a stogie factory
and the other because of the box and the difficult draw
and where he used to sit in the dark with a little
fire in front of his face and the peepers starting.

He adored the shad and gave advice on
how to catch it and how to cook it and where
the runs were and how it tasted after eight
hours of roasting and you could eat it whole
because the bones had dissolved and what the oil
did for your heart and what it did for your skin.

And why Italians lived so long, and Jews,
if they stuck to their own diet, not forgetting
cucumbers, and how if you took a Dutchman who
lived in the city and worked in a store and fed him
the way you did his father and his grandfather
who ate at 7 A.M. how he would die
before he was fifty, and plants the same, and raccoons,
and Japanese most of all; and how love was
identical, if you loved a woman in her fifties

the same way you did when she was twenty and you were
thirty-eight what she would say and how the

winner of last year's shad festival forced a piece
of steel along the backbone to deceive the
judges at their scale, handkerchiefs, I guess
over their eyes, and how my love is thirty and
I am in my forties calling from a public
phone and I am haranguing her and we will be
crying together in less than an hour and arguing
about the moon and eating at 3 A.M., she
wanted leftover chicken and cold rice
and I had to walk downstairs in the dark and stopped
to read a line from Emily Dickinson and write
a note to her, Dear Love, and how this winter was
weird as winters go and how this life was
long, you can believe it, and how I labored.

He Said

Thank God for summer, he said, and thank God the window
was to his right and there was a wavy motion
behind him and a moon in the upper right corner
only four days old and still not either blowsy
or soupy.
          Thank God he was sitting, he said,
with his feet up on a rubber hose half-facing
a morning glory, the last, or the first, and thanks
for the ledge, he said, to put his coffee cup on
and the bush for his *Inquirer* and the watering can
and the pot of red petunias.
          And for that drain
and its sixty-one holes and its small black metal ridges
and the bug that wanders back and forth and the leaf
that somehow rests on the sand between the bricks
and the stack of wood and the green plastic garbage bags
that act as a carpet.
          And Blake the poet, he said,
a dove both black and white, and Moondog whom he watched
night after night in the early fifties playing
his instruments and moaning, and Amos, he said,
placed by the Gideons over the flowerpots,
who hated coldness, accommodation, extortion, oppression,
and roared in the grapes, he said, and melted mountains.

Index of Titles and First Lines